GERANIUMS — The Successful Grower's Guide

Geraniums –

The Successful Grower's Guide

MONICA BENNETT

John Bartholomew and Son Ltd,
Edinburgh.

First published in 1972 by
John Bartholomew and Son Ltd
Duncan Street,
Edinburgh. EH9 1TA

ISBN 0-85152-901-1

Printed in Great Britain by
Bristol Typesetting Co. Ltd.,
Barton Manor, St. Philips, Bristol

CONTENTS

FOREWORD

By H. Wood, Hon. Secretary of the
British Pelargonium and Geranium Society

IT is not necessary for me to eulogise too much on
the merits of Monica Bennett as a writer, breeder, and
grower of plants of the Pelargonium genus because she
is so very well known for her practical knowledge and
pleasant way of compiling authentic facts into easy
reading matter.

I would like, however, to give some words in brief
recommendation of this much awaited book and would
like to emphasise that such a book as this is very much
wanted owing to the author's perception of the subject.

Many gardening books seem to be written by journal-
ists who only research into other material that has been
written and they in themselves do not have the necessary first-hand experience for writing on a given specialist subject, such books and authors do little to make
available useful knowledge to people who need this,
most people read books for the purpose of increasing
their learning power, if the author can not fulfill this
need then he fails completely.

The author of this book has a number of very lovely
hybrids to her credit in the following pages and I
consider her to be one of the top authorities in the
country on the Geraniaceae family of plants.

I know that the whole of the author's life has been

with growing plants in which one can perceive her veritable love of horticulture in all its phases, this is clearly shown in the contents of the following chapters.

This inherent love of plants and nature is in many people for which they must be eternally grateful.

Henry G. Wood

INTRODUCTION

THIS book is the result of an inspiration born of the constant encouragement of friends in the geranium world (Mr. J. Wood in particular), of my devotion to the plants, and of the loving forbearance of my family who so completely understand my dedication. It is a tribute to the enthusiasm of growers everywhere, and to the countless friendships that I have made all over the world through the medium of writing, lecturing, judging and growing geraniums, and from the tremendous source of interest sustained through membership of The British Pelargonium and Geranium Society, The South African Pelargonium and Geranium Society, The Australian Geranium Society and the International Geranium Society, America.

During recent years there has been a great effort made to classify all geraniums as Pelargoniums, but some traditional prejudice has arisen in the trade, which refuses acceptance of such, as Pelargoniums have always been recognised as 'regals' and the geraniums as 'zonals'.

As this book is directed chiefly towards the amateur, to avoid any possible confusion, the botanical Pelargonium will be referred to throughout as the geranium in keeping with the common usage within the trade.

Here then, is my book affectionately presented in the hope that it will further stimulate increasing interest in the fascinating world of geraniums and pelargoniums.

Monica Bennett

A*

GERANIUMS FOR ALL

ALTHOUGH the geranium was actually introduced to the world of horticulture sometime during the seventeenth century, it made its real debut in English gardens when Europe was groping in the turmoil and dissention of the Napoleonic age. It lent vivid colour to summer beds during the long stormy days of the great industrial revolution, and by the time that history was caught up in the Victorian reign, it had soared to a peak of favour previously undreamed of.

Then about the middle of the eighteenth century, France produced the embryo of the double geranium, and hybridists were already at work on the species, with the result that in even more varied form the geranium continued to brighten formal gardens and public layouts, and to provide pot plants for window sills of country cottages. It did indeed seem that the humble plant that possessed such gaiety had come to stay, unmoved by the changing time of man, and that it was destined to remain extremely fashionable. Certainly the agony of the Boer War was reflected in its glaring redness in both park and private garden, and it began to assume an almost stereotyped pattern that strangely lacked some of the excitement it had at first offered.

It survived the dreadful upheaval of the First World War, but its flamboyancy diminished somewhat in the tremendous drive for food production, and for the first time the pedestal of the geranium tottered as the spotlight moved to the vegetable kingdom.

By the end of the war, it was beginning to lose favour, although it had the ability to present a very patriotic blending in combination with the ubiquitous lobelia and alyssum, but a new way of life was opening up . . . new ideas and approaches . . . and in a changing world struggling back to sanity from the aftermath of a desolating war, the slow but sure decline of the geranium unhappily began. . . .

Suddenly the blatant red was too harsh for the more artistic trend towards gardening in general, and to most people the geranium, sinking into the background of partial obscurity, was just another vivid flower of little matter or portent. But the strength of public opinion, even in the vast field of horticulture, is undermined and shattered by the restless winds of demand, and quietly hybridists continued to work and produce new varieties which broke new ground in colour and form, and a slow but insistent infiltration commenced, that was to carry the geranium on a great tidal wave of popularity that now has no limits, and has extended world wide.

CHAPTER I

GERANIUM HISTORY

In the spacious fields of horticulture, there eventually comes a time when every type of plant is caught up in a welter of technical and scientific data, which often reaches out far beyond the normal comprehension of the ordinary layman seeking practical knowledge, and presents such a confusion of thought to him that floundering helplessly in the advanced complications of modern theory, he tires, and seeks a course of retreat rather than attempt to work out the issues.

The geranium, belonging to the family *Geraniaceae* is such a real down to earth subject, that in simple terms, I hope to infuse new enthusiasm in the hearts of all gardeners in a most determined effort to make even more popular, a plant that has no limits, and certainly no frustrating temperament.

The habitat of the geranium was South Africa, and in the seventeenth century it suddenly made an appearance in England and gained a foothold. It was during the Victorian era that it made a most remarkable impact on the public, and became widely accepted in parks, gardens, conservatories, and country cottages, where the blatant, brilliant colour dominated the scene, and strangely enough then, the geranium was associated only with this startling shade of red.

After the First World War, the geranium took a dramatically steep slide in loss of favour, largely because strictly formal landscapes were no longer the

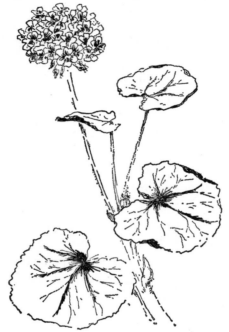

Pelargonium inquinans

trend. A partial eclipse obscured the zonal geranium, and it was mostly the regal, or pelargonium, or Lady Washington geraniums as they are known in America which continued to grace the window sills. The zonal was not quite so desirable because of its close association with lobelia and allysum as a bedding trio which had somehow become traditional, and there was a growing urge amongst the more contemporary gardeners to make a clean break away.

The geranium certainly looked like falling into the inevitable abyss of horticultural failures, despite the fact that there was an assortment of varieties available, although the public majority seemed unaware and disinterested in the existence of such. The whole horizon of the geranium world seemed to comprise of Crampel, Gustave Emich, and King of Denmark, a formidable trio that have weathered the long years, and still maintain a constant demand today, after the great revival that built up some time during the 1930s.

Pelargonium peltatum

Although the geranium had received a severe set back, some hybridists who were enthusiastic, dedicated and diligent, continued to quietly persevere with their great work of crossing and back crossing, and new and exciting varieties began to make a subtle appearance, not hailed with much advance publicity, but with sufficient dominance to very slowly reverse the lamentable adversity that had strangely befallen this most ubiquitous plant.

Interest was growing by such a rate, that in 1952, The National Geranium Society came into being (much later to be known as The British Pelargonium and Geranium Society) and some coherency was at last brought to bear upon the chaos of nomenclature which had hitherto prevailed ; a task that could only have been undertaken by true geranium lovers. Now there was some purpose, and a goal in the world of the pelargonium and geranium, there were new horizons and, vast

Pelargonium tricolor

scope for experimental work, plus an exhilarating future that had no limits or confines.

The geranium had reached the heights it so richly

deserved, and the upsurge of its sudden incredible popularity was like a great resurrection. It had arrived in a progressive age of horticulture, and gardening trends, that could provide it with the honour and dignity it so well merited.

The geranium was nationally and internationally acclaimed!

CHAPTER 2

GERANIUM TYPES

IT is tiring to the novice or layman to become involved at first in technical terms regarding the subdivision of the geranium in groups. The more simple and straight forward the initiation, the greater the interest that will be stimulated. In actual fact, the principal types most generally known are Zonals, Ivy leaved, Scented, Irenes and Regals, and these can further be couched without any confusion into an extension quite easy to define as we progress.

Zonals can consist of single, semi-double and double varieties, and are so headed because the leaf normally had a distinct zone or darker marking, but in many modern varieties, this has little bearing because some of the foliage is almost plain. A typical example of a zonal with well marked foliage is the old Paul Crampel, and a modern zonal with practically no trace of the original zone is Plato.

Foliage of an old type zonal with strong markings

A single variety consists of a floret or pip having five petals, although this cannot be adamantly standard-ised because sometimes a six petalled floret will be produced.

SEMI DOUBLE AND DOUBLES

There is no concise demarkation between semi double and double, and it is very often difficult even for the professional to confidently decide which is which. The plants are usually shorter jointed, more fleshy and stocky, and the flowers do not shatter so easily, with the result that they are often used for floral arrangements and for wreath work. The flowers last a fortnight in water when cut. They open to perfection in the summer, but even in warmth, the trusses are usually poorly formed in the winter with curling petals, and some types do not produce any flowers at all. The more tightly double they are, (a typical example being the Rosebuds) the more difficult to even expect a flower in the dormant months.

Invariably the single zonal is preferred to the double because of its clear, startling beauty, but in the summer, the massive trusses of doubles like Irene and her progeny, and the compact, ball-like heads of Jewel, really come into their own in no uncertain way, and dazzle the eye with their sheer glory.

CACTUS

By no means a dominant group, this, but very appealing when grown purely as pot plants, for they have the capacity to flower themselves almost to death. The plants are on the wiry side, with small foliage, and the trusses are small, the petals being rolled or quilled. A good example is the brilliant signal red Firedragon, and the appealing pink Mrs. Salter Bevis.

AMERICAN GERANIUMS

These are really on their own, the most famous being the illustrious Irenes and the ever widening range. They are double and semi double, strong, stocky plants with vigorous foliage, bearing huge heads of flowers, making fine pot plants, and excellent for bedding, especially in a dry season.

VARIEGATED GERANIUMS

Under this heading we get all types of geraniums which may be grown principally for foliage effect, because with many of them the flowers are of little import, often being small and comparatively insignificant, but the leaves are so decorative that they more than compensate for floral deficiencies, although hybridists have made a successful breakthrough with some fine new ones like Gaiety Girl, Dollar Princess, Golden Atom, Barbara Clark and Prince Regent which bear very large trusses.

The most popular and beautiful must surely be the tricolour Mr. H. Cox with pale green foundation suffused with darker green, red, cream and gold. The flowers are often removed because they are uninteresting. This variety is becoming scarce and a little variable in some parts of the country. Good stock should be taken care of and propagated well.

An example of butterfly marked foliage is A Happy Thought. Each light green leaf bears a cream marking exactly the shape of a butterfly, and sometimes the plant bears ' ghosts ' which are pale cream shoots and leaves entirely lacking in chlorophyll.

The silver leaved group including Caroline Schmidt, Mrs. Parker and Spitfire have grey-green foliage with silver or cream edging, and the dark foliaged varieties like Monica Bennett and Black Vesuvius have almost black-green leaves with intense zones.

Distinction is a classic example of pencil marking – a thin dark zone clearly defined on each leaf.

Verona is the type known as the golden leaved, used extensively in designs for outdoor bedding. The foliage is yellow.

Chocolate zoning is typified by His Majesty, and is very distinctive. A rather unique variegated geranium is Miss Burdett Coutts, which lacks chlorophyll to such an extent that growth is slow, and practically dormant during the winter.

All variegated geraniums require plenty of light, and not too much nitrogenous feeding, or the brilliance of the colouring will be lost.

IVY LEAVED VARIETIES

This group of geraniums used largely for hanging baskets, window boxes, and for trailing from shelves, or training up canes, have single, double and semi-double flowers borne in profusion, but all have the ivy-shaped leaves which gives them their name. In fact L'Elegante is so much like a hedera, that it is often mistaken for one, especially as the leaves are variegated.

They are far more brittle stemmed than the Zonals, breaking easily at the joints, and flower formation is loose. They climb only if given support, therefore the natural habit is prostrate. Some wonderful specimens have been shown where plants have been expertly trained over wire cages three feet high, and the ultimate result has been quite eye catching.

IVY HYBRIDS

The hybrids are crosses between the ivy leaf and the zonals, and I consider are much more exciting. They carry the virtues of both parents, and are more robust. The habit is partially prostrate and partially erect, so that they are ideal for training up canes. The flowers are better than those of the ivy leaf. Two examples are Forest Maid with compact red flowers and the lovely Millfield Gem with solid heavy trusses, but all are well worth growing.

SCENTED GERANIUMS

Whilst not so popular as the other groups, the scented varieties have a very special charm of their own, especially when they are like the enchanting Mabel Gray with its aromatic scent of crushed lemons and lime, or Fragrans with its delicate citrus perfume. Most of them have small flowers similar in shape to those of the Regal pelargonium. There is no set pattern as regards foliage, and size and form varies.

MINIATURE· AND DWARF TYPES

Quite definitely becoming the trend. The range has increased considerably, and embraces some fascinating introductions. The plants are very short and compact, and the miniatures extremely slow in growth. They make excellent pot plants for the home and greenhouse decoration. Foliage varies from blackish green to very light shades, and flower formation is quite assorted. Trusses are minute on the miniatures, larger on the dwarfs, but few can resist these babies of the geranium world.

SPECIES

A most interesting group for the collector, or for anyone who likes an unusual plant. A typical example, and certainly my favourite because of its unpredictability is that almost grotesque *P. gibbosum* with swollen joints which lends it the nickname of Gouty geranium. In the summer my specimen plant became my despair losing all its leaves, yet reprieved itself from an ignominious end because it continued to flower with umbels of lemon-green blossom, scentless by day, bewitching by night, then during the winter, produced a new crop of foliage, and became a most handsome subject with a ridiculous freshness for the time of the year. I was enslaved all over again.

REGAL PELARGONIUMS

The regals are totally different from the zonals, insofar as the leaves are palmate, rough and wrinkled, and the flowers very showy, each pip having petunia form, and most of them are suffused with other colours. The pelargoniums have been known for at least 150 years, but hybridisers have made tremendous strides in the evolution of this species, and from small flowers, they have graduated to immense blooms, a few of the modern varieties being nearly four inches in diameter. They are mass bloomers in May and June, and for the rest of the season are more or less spasmodic. A continuity of young plants will maintain a sequence of flowers, but unlike the zonal, they refuse a display during the winter. The pelargoniums are used mainly as pot plants, but they will flower quite happily outside in the summer.

CHAPTER 3

PROPAGATION

THE whole range of geraniums can be propagated vegetatively, and by seed, but far and away the best method for the amateur is by the former, because with cuttings, the results are quicker and less complicated. The young plants grow and flower well in the same season, whereas if seed is sown, apart from the Carefree group, there will be no flowering until the following season. Furthermore cuttings are quite true to type, whereas seeds are not, so that a crop from seed sowing could well be disappointing and very frustrating.

Actually it is only where new introductions are required, or where an amateur is really interested in hybridising, that seed will be used. At one time tradition governed horticulture very dominantly and this extended even to geraniums, and the rules were that all cuttings should be severed from the parent plant with a sharp knife or razor blade, that they should be about three inches long and trimmed to just below a leaf axil before insertion. The modern approach is more exploratory, and now leaf axil and tip cuttings are freely taken, especially with new varieties where speedy propagation of such is necessary, and personally I believe that the most hygienic method of taking cuttings is by breaking them off. As with chrysanthemum cuttings, there is far less risk in transmitting disease from plant to plant, and with the thousands of ' cuttings ' I take each year, I never use a knife. Conflicting statements from carping critics would suggest that a break will leave a ragged wound that almost invites botrytis spores to enter, and commence the progressive dying back of the parent stem, but this can happen just as easily where severance has been made with a knife. In actual fact it is mainly during the winter months that there is any real danger of this trouble occurring, and it only occurs in the greenhouse when conditions favour such eruptions, like excessive damp or low sluggish temperatures. In any case, very few amateurs would take cuttings in the dormant months.

The use of hormones with geranium cuttings is very debatable, because normally there is sufficient hereditary hormones present to subsidise the cutting in the initial stages and carry it safely through the process of rooting, and I would not consider the application of such as a necessity. It could well amount to a matter of personal choice.

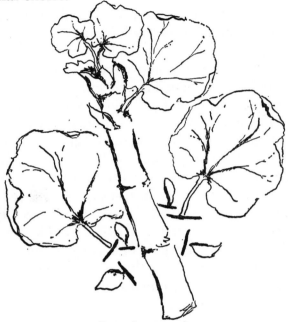

Preparing a cutting

Remove the stipules (these are the leafy bits that form at the leaf axles) for this rots and can set up black leg when the cuttings are rooting. Remove also the lower leaves because they are an added strain during the period when roots are forming, but do not denude the cuttings. There is an age old theory that all cuttings should be left for a few days before inserting in the medium, so that the ends can callouse over, and it is still practised today, but it is a fallacy, and I would never advise it, because severe wilting follows and then the cuttings have to struggle to recover from the effects at the same time that they are trying to make root causing an unnecessary burden. The cuttings can be placed immediately they are taken into the rooting medium.

A prepared cutting

There are countless methods of rooting cuttings. A cable heated propagator is ideal set at 60 degrees F, but applied heat is only necessary during the winter months, and the majority of amateurs would obviously avoid this period. The cuttings only require moisture for rooting which makes the hydroponic system ideal (the growing in dilute feed solutions allied to the soilless culture theory). Otherwise a medium of peat, soilless compost, or a mixture of half peat and half sharp grit will induce excellent root formation. In the early months of the year, rooting may take up to three weeks, but in the summer when there is a natural warmth, it is speedier, and ten days should see root development.

The novice with little facilities could use pots and put about half a dozen cuttings round the side, using the same medium, and potting singly as soon as rooted.

A humex propagator showing seedlings being raised on the right and soil warming on the left to assist the growth of young plants

There are many simple propagators now on the market, aimed at the novice, which consist of plastic seed trays with clear polystyrene tops to fit over with inlet ventilators. By long experiments I have found that geranium cuttings do like air when rooting, because they resent the close humidity of a propagating frame shut down. My 100 per cent success has been by keeping the frame open during the day and closing at night with just a crack of ventilation. With cable heating the medium dries out quickly when the frame is open, so every day, spray over with clean water.

Where cuttings are in pots or seed trays, be careful

not to over water. Ensure that the medium is moist, and that should be sufficient.

During the duller months shading is not necessary for the cuttings, but if propagating under glass when the sun has gained some power, there are times when it might be necessary to give some protection until the roots are established, and this can be done with sheets of paper. If rooting outside in the summer and early autumn, matters are considerably simplified, and the cuttings can be inserted in the open ground where they will root quite naturally.

Although pot grown plants can yield good and pro-lific cuttings, and are a surety under glass in case of storm damage or loss outside, there is no disputing that parent plants are more robust and strong when bedded in the open with complete freedom and unrestricted root run. They will put up tremendous vegetative growth sufficient to supply all needs, and the general constitution is much sounder and vigorous and certainly conducive to healthy stock.

The ideal time for the beginner to take cuttings is from July until mid September, but the earlier the better because the removal of stem cuttings will create a more bushy plant, giving enough time for fresh shoots to form to give the normal display of flowers outside.

Always propagate from healthy plants only. If there are any signs of malformation, distortion or stunted growth, avoid taking cuttings because it is only trans-mitting disease and building up trouble with stock. Con-stant re-selection of plants is advisable and all doubtful ones are best singled out and destroyed.

CHAPTER 4

COMPOST AND POTS FOR GERANIUMS

The word compost is no longer a traditional definition of soil (usually gleaned from the garden) wood ash, sand and secretive additions of various straight fertilisers. Science has entered this field to a very marked degree, and given form and stability to the compilation of excellent composts that can provide most of the plants' requirements during the span of life in pots or containers.

The advent of John Innes composts removed to a great extent the shroud of secrecy, and eliminated many of the mixtures which growers worked out to their personal experiments and theories, and we were at last presented with a standard formula, containing a variance only in the quantity of fertiliser added to give us a complete range of composts from No. 1 to 4 for every type of plant.

John Innes No. 1 is seven parts of sterilised, fibrous loam, three parts of peat, and two parts of coarse sand and crushed gravel, and to each bushel of this mixture, add $\frac{3}{4}$ ounces of chalk and $\frac{1}{4}$ lb of John Innes base fertiliser. No. 2 has the same ingredients with the exception that the fertiliser is doubled, and for No. 3 trebled and so on. This is all sufficient unto itself, and if the formula is not strictly adhered to, then the perfect balance can be materially upset. Supplementary feeds can always be applied later to plants which require additional nutrients as they develop and mature.

After the fertiliser has been added, John Innes composts should not be stored for longer than three months before using, as some chemical breakdown occurs due to bacterial activity.

Actually there is nothing to better a good loam based compost for geraniums, but with the increasing difficulty each year to obtain first class, top spit loam, the time must come when substitutes will have to be generally accepted by the majority of growers, and in these circumstances we shall have to turn hopefully to the soilless composts which have already reached the market with varying impact.

After prolonged and exacting trials with these new composts, I found that being peat based, they produced excellent root action, and were good for seedlings and cuttings, but there was not sufficient stability or body in the material for large matured plants which carried heavy growth like the American geraniums. The perfection of form and outline in a geranium lies in the compact, sturdy growth, and where soilless composts were used, it was jet propelled, tall, and top heavy, especially when used in conjunction with plastic pots.

A combination of equal parts of John Innes compost and soilless compost eased the matter somewhat, and brought about more satisfactory results.

Plants growing for a season in soilless composts later required weekly liquid feeds to replace the elements which had been leached from what was formerly a neutral material before the artificial impregnation of nutrients. After two months, all the plants could possibly obtain was moisture, and this led to a gradual deterioration in the geraniums until supplementary precision feeding was adopted. This is the main difference which exists between loam based and peat based composts.

In John Innes formulae, plants would grow through a whole season without additional feed if the grower happened to be ignorant of the requirements, or just plain neglectful, and I, myself, have had stock plants in large pots for five years, which have only received an occasional top dressing, and a few feeds, yet growth has been commendably sustained.

Greater detail has to be given to the care of geraniums in soilless composts as regards watering, and I found a much higher incidence of black leg occurring in well-established plants in $3\frac{1}{2}$ inch and even 5 inch pots, due, I assumed, to the fact that too much moisture was retained too long. Personally I cannot ever remember losing a plant through this cause when grown in John Innes composts.

But the days of the soilless composts are with us undeniably, and the field of experimental work is still wide open for further and urgent exploration. We can look optimistically to the perhaps very near future when science will be able to cry ' eureka ' and we shall suddenly have the answer to the quest for the perfect compost.

There was a time too, and not so far distant either, when clay pots were considered a ' must ' for geraniums.

Pelargonium The Doctor

Three 1972 seedlings awaiting registration

Dwarf Amanda Jane

Tradition in horticulture rises occasionally like an in-surmountable barrier which stoutly resists the infusion of anything approaching a sensational change. Modern methods, if they are really drastic and effect some sweeping changes, are viewed with great suspicion and prejudice, insomuch that a battle has to wage during which criticism and personal experiences are bandied to and fro until at last visual proof gives indisputable tangibility. Only then is the finger of progress allowed to slowly move, but still the minority cling steadfastly to the remnants of their faith and belief, refusing acceptance of the new way of life.

So it was with the introduction of the plastic pot with its non-porosity, its cleanliness, greater warmth and complete hygiene. It took a few years to batten down the storm of controversy that swelled against its use, but gradually reason asserted itself, and practically the whole of the horticultural trade turned over to the new world of plastics which now embraces seed trays, propagators, bulb bowls, gravel trays, tomato

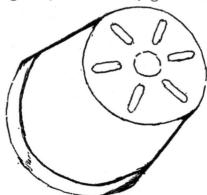

A plastic pot showing the drainage holes

B

rings and watering cans to name but a few of the commodities available.

I was personally involved with experiments during the pioneering of the plastic pot, and complete success was achieved with growing geraniums and pelargoniums in plastics, provided that watering was moderate, because the moisture was retained much longer in the pots. Possibly one of the greatest advantages is that plastic pots are five degrees warmer, which is worth considering during the winter and early spring. I would not use clay pots again because they could well be conveyors of disease with their accumulative algae and dirt.

There is a wide range of colour in plastics which can meet the most trendy choice, but I prefer the plain terra cotta for geraniums. When growing from cuttings to first potting, there are an assortment of cheap pots including whalehide, peat, papiermâché and polythene, and all serve the same purpose, although sometimes they are very temporary, probably lasting about three months. In any case, by that time plants will require re-potting.

There is a varying quality in plastic pots, but the price will more or less act as a guide, and with a keenly competitive market, the days of the clay pots are numbered. Only extremely conservative gardeners will continue to use them in the future, and stockists will be few and far between.

CHAPTER 5

GERANIUMS IN POTS

PROBABLY as many geraniums today are grown in pots for display in conservatories, verandas, greenhouses and the home, as are planted outside. It is therefore important to know just how to treat the plants during the season if the very best results are to be obtained.

There are far too many growers who cherish the idea that the geranium must be pot bound or kept close to a starvation diet to bring it to maximum flowering capacity. Any plant which has to struggle for its existence, hastens to complete its life cycle before obliteration, and in its slow deterioration, concentrates on flowering and seeding. A good example of this process is with bedding plants, which, if kept too long in the boxes and starved of nutrients, will give a mass of flowers, then begin to die down. If the geranium is meted out such treatment, it will never be seen at its best. That is why it is often difficult to identify poorly grown plants which are never capable of producing well formed trusses to their maximum size.

There are countless growers who have not the facilities for carrying on their plants into larger pots, and for lack of space are compelled to confine them to the small sizes. In cases like this, regular feeds will have to be applied and it helps considerably if the pots can be stood on an aggregate of gravel similar to that which is used for ring culture of tomatoes. If plants are in the house, they can be stood on a tray with moist gravel. I would not recommend this method apart from circumstances such as this, because I do not favour it for mobile plants. Once the roots get well out in the gravel and establish themselves, they have to be wrenched out when the plants are moved to another position, and I feel that it is a shock to the whole constitution of the plants. All my geraniums are thoroughly mobile and stand on dry wooden staging, and the roots contain themselves within the confines of the pots.

To reach perfection with geraniums in pots, it is advisable to adopt methods similar to that employed with chrysanthemums, going from 3½ inches to 5½ inches and from there to 8 inches, but the compost differs insofar as John Innes No. 1 and No. 2 are sufficient, and it is only occasionally that No. 3 is used for the stronger and bolder varieties.

A rooted cutting

As soon as the cuttings are rooted, and this becomes very obvious by the fresh appearance of the leaves, they should be carefully removed from the medium. I say carefully, because the new roots are brittle and tear away easily. Using a soilless or John Innes No. 1 compost transfer to 3½ inch pots, using thumb pressure only to firm.

If the compost is on the dry side, water afterwards, and stand the pots so that they are not packed too closely. It is essential that air and light can get freely to the plants, and space is necessary for development.

Do not over water, especially if it is early in the year when potting is undertaken. When one has mastered the art of the watering can he is assured of the greater measure of success, because so much can accrue from not understanding the needs of the plants as regards moisture. Too much water, or even too little, can result in yellowing leaves and a general deterioration. Even more care must be exercised if a combination of plastic pots and soilless compost is used. It is natural for the compost to retain moisture longer, and also for the pots to retain it being non-porous, with the unhappy result that if there is continual wetness with no drying out at all, even established plants will damp off or show signs of black leg. Experimenting in this direction I found that Mr. Henry Cox, Miss Burdett Coutts and Maxim Kovelesky quickly reacted in this way, and it is obvious that some of the weaker growing varieties resent too much moisture as the roots cannot absorb it in quantity.

No trouble at all was experienced with John Innes compost in plastic pots, and amongst the thousands of plants that I have grown not one single maturing plant has gone down with black leg.

A large trial batch of the hardy old Paul Crampel standing in 3½ inch pots awaiting bedding out time, having been grown from cuttings right through in soil-less compost, had a large number of casualties which caused considerable concern, because it was something that had not been experienced before, and it was only the fact that a similar number growing in John Innes compost remained in perfect condition, that I was able to pinpoint the cause of the trouble.

The problem could then be counteracted by judicious

A well-rooted cutting in a correct size pot

watering, and this is definitely the basic step in the modern approach to growing geraniums to perfection.

As soon as the plants are about six inches high, they

will in all probability, show signs of running upwards with a single stem, so to create some shape and bushiness, they should be pinched at the top close to a node, and the shoot thus removed could in turn be used as a cutting. This operation will induce branching, and it can be repeated later on at the tip of each new stem when sufficient growth has been made, which is desirable when growing for maximum display and for exhibition.

Geraniums should never be over potted, and only when the roots have worked out and encompassed the existing ball of compost, and this is usually assessable by the size and vigour of the plants, is it time to make a move into 5 or $5\frac{1}{2}$ inch pots, using John Innes No. 2, or the equivalent in any other medium.

Be certain not to overpot, like this example

The plant should have been watered half an hour prior to the move if it was dry, and then it slips easily

1. Place the hand over the pot, with the stem between the middle fingers

2. Invert the pot and tap the base

3. Place the root ball in a size larger pot and refill with fresh compost

from the pot without a break down of the ball of soil. Place about half an inch of fresh compost in the bottom of the pot (if plastic ones are used, no drainage is necessary) and set the plant in the centre, then carefully place the new compost evenly around, pressing down with a narrow dibber for preference, not too hard, but firmer than in the 3½ inch pots so that there are no air pockets or gaps.

Space the plants out so that the leaves do not touch others in surrounding pots. Where room is very limited, this will not be possible, but it is most important now for an availability of plenty of air and light. A temperature of 45 to 50 degrees F is all that is required for steady, healthy growth. In the early part of the year, high temperatures and dull days contribute largely to leggy, untidy growth which is undesirable. When the plants are young and approaching bud stage, I often spray them lightly with clean water late in the afternoon (never when frost is in the air) and it is surprising how fresh and happy they look the next day. All my young plants are watered overhead in the early stages.

Before the flowers are out, I foliar spray once a fortnight, and this seems to put some body into the foliage.

If display or stock plants are required, and we always grow a large number in pots for this purpose to enable cuttings to be taken the year round, then the final move is into 8 or 8½ inch pots, and I invariably use again John Innes No. 2, although this could be a matter for the grower to personally decide. There is no hard and fast rule, and I know a first class Scottish grower, who always final pots with No. 3, and her plants are well

B*

beyond the pale of criticism. Of course, maximum light and a wonderful clean environment in the Highlands, is vastly different from producing plants in the drab industrial midlands, so this is taken into account.

The procedure now is much the same as before, only even firmer potting is essential to give the plants the stability they require, and it may be necessary later to insert thin canes to support some of the stems, especially if they bear heavy heads of flowers like some of the American varieties, where the sheer weight can cause a breakage. The canes should be discreetly concealed if possible so that they do not detract from the plant. For geraniums I prefer the two-foot split bamboo canes.

The lifetime of the geranium in a pot is assumed by many to be about two years, but this generalisation can be ignored to a great degree, because I have had plants in large pots for as long as six years. Cutting them back early each spring, they branch out afresh in gentle heat and give a glory of flowers each season. Top dressings, foliar feeds and supplementary liquid feeds during the summer kept them in really good condition. However in most cases, geraniums spend about two years in pots, and are either broken down for cuttings, or the following summer are transferred to the open ground for a display, then in the autumn the last crop of cuttings are taken, and the old plants destroyed as they are uprooted for ground clearance. This actually is fully advocated in the interest of plant hygiene.

All geraniums give of their best as regards flowering in pots, and glass house protection produces the ultimate in truss perfection.

Making a bushy plant

Opening out the plant

Pinching out

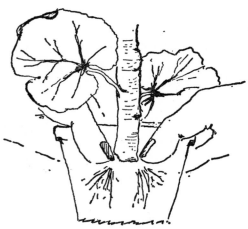

Too much pressure when repotting could cause root fracture !

CHAPTER 6

DWARFS AND MINIATURES AS POT PLANTS

IN recent years the popularity of dwarf and miniature geraniums has shown a most remarkable ascendancy, and their virtues lie in a tremendous capacity for flowering, which overrides the fact that petals shatter and drop freely. They are compact, slow growing, with complete adaptability as house plants and for display in limited spaces.

The dwarf varieties rarely exceed a height of about ten to twelve inches, and the stems are short jointed, with small neat foliage. A typical example is my own namesake, Monica Bennett, with its bushy growth and amazing florescence which is continuous throughout the summer and spasmodic in the winter. It retains its petals well too.

The dwarfs bed very well outside, and are ideal for a narrow border or even the rockery, but it is as pot plants that they excel.

Potting on is a much slower process than with the large geraniums, and in actual fact, a dwarf will spend most of its lifetime in a pot no larger than a five inch, providing that nutrients are applied as required to keep it reasonably healthy. Some growers prefer to confine them to small pots, and this is a good idea if a large collection is desired, and space has become a problem.

It is rare that the plants have to be stopped to encourage side shoots to develop, and usually the removal of cuttings is sufficient to maintain shapeliness.

Tom Thumb with its neat light green foliage, and masses of dainty pink flowers with white eye is always attractive, even in the winter but it is advisable to stop this one occasionally to prevent untidiness. A very easy geranium with no peculiarities and extremely tolerant. Probably that is why it has survived 100 years!

Golden Harry Hieover or Alpha as it is often known, is very delightful, having light foliage with a pronounced chestnut zone. The flowers are small, single and bright vermilion, and there is a tendency for the plant to be pendulous.

Very appealing is Blakesdorf with sage green leaves and black zone, offset by single orange red flowers, and equally as alluring is Friesdorf with small dark foliage and a profusion of geranium lake trusses with narrow petals. Both have a tremendous capacity for a rich display and unrivalled popularity.

Into the beginners collection I would most certainly place Red Black Vesuvius with very compact dark foliage and bright red single flowers, Monica Bennett, again with rich, dark, well zoned leaves and pale lilac flowers borne en masse over a prolonged period, Flash with its bright single scarlet trusses with base of petals white, and Timothy Clifford with double salmon flowers set against dark green foliage.

As white geraniums are becoming the vogue, they must be included and it would be very difficult to make a selection out of that great trio, Virgo, White Gem and Wood's White.

Twinkle is a bushy plant that grows very well, and the double coral rose trusses are bright and gay against the dark leaves, and for something a little unusual there is Red Spider with most intense red flowers that have twisted petals.

The enchanting Wilheim Hertzog is a dual purpose variety with light green leaves and semi-double scarlet flowers, which makes it admirable as a pot plant, or it can be used very effectively for bedding, because growth is not too slow.

Very lovely is Nadine with yellowish leaves bearing dominant bronze which is a splendid foil for the double dawn pink flowers. It should rank high in the charts for dwarf geranium popularity, because few can resist it.

Emma Hossler is most dependable, well established, fast growing as a dwarf with charming double rose-pink trusses blending perfectly with the light foliage.

Some of the American introductions are likely to prove extremely trendy, and I certainly recommend Altair with olive green leaves and double coral flowers, very easy of growth and quick.

Night and Day is aptly named because the leaves are very dark, and the flowers have a white foundation lightly flushed with pale pink. Miniatures are naturally rather slow for propagating, because vegetatively they make very little growth, especially when confined to the smaller pots, and that is why the price is stable. The dwarfer a plant, the more costly it is because reproduction is very retarded compared to other types.

If the diminutive charm of the miniatures is to be retained, they should never be over potted, but at the same time they must not be relegated to a starvation diet. Over potting can lead to rotting off and only when the roots bind the ball of compost, and it is obvious that the plants are becoming pot bound, should they be moved on to another size, but I rarely go beyond a 4 or 4½ inch. During the winter the plants make very little progress and seem to remain unchanging.

The flowers are profuse, and borne clear of the foliage, and there is a wide variation in colour, but despite the present day trend towards miniatures, I cannot foresee them topping the geranium world by a long measure, because they will always remain largely for the collector, rather than the average grower. A genuine effort has been made to give publicity to these fascinating babies, and bring the pendulum of popularity swinging in their favour, but they will have difficulty reaching the dizzy heights recorded by the progressively challenging zonals which are completely all-purpose.

For the time being, the miniatures are caught up in a whirlpool of fashion . . . they are a vogue which faces the perpetual possibility of partial eclipse, and tenaciously sustained by a minority of almost fanatical enthusiasts. They are slow, and this is the age of jet speed . . . they are not madly flamboyant, and these are the days of gay scintillation but they can nevertheless be intriguing.

Fantasie, a brilliant pure white, with medium green foliage and very compact habit is the best white I have seen, and very few could resist Gay Baby, the tiny ivy leaf variety with pale mauve flowers. I have a plant growing out of the bottom of a wine bottle hanging up, and although growth is painfully slow, it has been in flower for nine months.

Enchanting is the only word to describe Sweet Sue, the mandarin red flowers of which have a large white eye, flushed purple-pink. The leaves are green, and it makes an irresistible pot plant.

Kewensis has quite a following, and in a moderate climate it beds very well, but the newer Silver Kewensis is a real gem with single crimson flowers that glow against the green and white variegated leaves.

Sunstar is very appealing because it is like a baby Orangesonne, and even the unusual shaped foliage of its parent is a replica in every detail. The flower is a double bright orange and quite distinctive. Another attractive miniature is Taurus which has narrow petalled flowers supported well above the foliage in slender stems. It is rich salmon and the leaves are mid green with the black blotch in the centre, very like The Boar. It could well be a winner because it is definitely a little out of the ordinary.

I like Vasco Da Gama, a rather formidable name for the first miniature Irene, but it is lovely, and like a cameo of its illustrious parent. It could be very popular indeed, and a rosy future could well be assured for Variegated Kleine Leibling. It is slow, and the foliage is mid green with crinkled white edges. Very floriferous, the flowers are single, pink with upper petals based white. A delightful combination.

A first class miniature is Orion, a continuously flowering orange-red double with dark foliage and very bushy habit. It cannot help but be a top liner, and given favourable conditions, it makes a wonderful house plant, colourful and gay.

Catford Belle, the miniature regal is very pretty with neat, compact foliage, and pale purple flowers, the upper petals generously marked with deep purple. It is very floriferous and is a fine pot plant. It is a pity that there are not many more miniature regals.

The American Party Dress is a great favourite of mine, so I particularly like its tiny replica, Denebola raised by that expert miniature hybridist, the Rev. S. Stringer. It is a violet-pink semi-double with a white centre to the florets. The doubles and semi-doubles do not shatter so easily.

Imp is a pretty salmon, as impish as its name implies, and completely adorable, and the list of varieties grow each season as more hybridisers work enthusiastically upon the miniatures.

There will be a natural impulse to produce smaller and smaller types, until a magnifying glass or microscope will be required to view them in detail, and this will be the race of micro-miniatures.

CHAPTER 7

GERANIUMS FOR DISPLAY AND BEDDING

THERE is a delightful versatility about the geranium which makes it almost indispensable for bedding during the summer. No longer is it necessary to tolerate the monotony of the red Crampel, for the colour range is now extensive providing an outlet for some fascinating designs in the flower beds. There are few plants which yield such a continuity of bloom from planting out time until frosts terminate their floriferance, and their adaptability is such that they will give of their best in practically any type of soil and condition, happily contending with the pollution of industrial areas and fume drenched traffic islands, revelling in parks and town gardens and bringing much needed brightness where otherwise it would be drab.

Over the years Paul Crampel, probably the best known of all geraniums has received an infusion under its name of close seedlings bearing a similarity, which have been marketed by indiscriminate growers as Crampels, and this has helped to bring a deterioration in some stocks, and a deplorable reflection on the otherwise superb qualities of the original Crampel. This is one of the sad things about geraniums, which we sincerely hope will eventually be eradicated, and hybridists have worked hard to bring out an improved strain of Crampel which is easily distinguishable by excellent colour, large trusses, stocky plants and well zoned foliage. A genuine Crampel should not have small pips and trusses and variable colour, with straggly growth.

It was wrongly assumed at one time that few other varieties would bed out satisfactorily apart from the variegated types like Mrs. H. Cox, Caroline Schmidt and His Majesty, but it has been proved that practically every known kind will settle down to outdoor life in the summer, apart from heavy, solid doubles like Mrs. A. M. Mayne which dislike too much wet. Whites have long been a problem in the Black Country especially, but I have raised an excellent, strong growing variety, Staple White, which never becomes tarnished even in our locality, and flowers with perfect form all through the winter under glass.

Variegated geraniums show an intensity of colour when grown outside and this intensity is never reached in a greenhouse. A splendid show would be assured by planting any of the following; Dolly Varden, a silver tri-colour with vivid red single flowers, Happy Thought, having a green leaf with a cream butterfly in the centre, and bright cherry red flowers, Mrs. Parker, cream edged bi-colour leaf with very pretty double rose trusses, Spitfire with cream and green variegated foliage similar to Schmidt, but bearing red cactus flowers in profusion, and Mrs. Strang with grand tri-colour leaves very like Mrs. Cox.

Most people are familiar with that superb old Maxim Koveleski and its fine single orange trusses that stand the weather so well, but equally as durable, with magnificent heads of perfectly formed pips is Brutus, a glowing orange red with strong growth.

Other outstanding singles are Francis James, a white with unusual plum red eye and picotee edge, Pandora, a first class red with well zoned leaves, Plato, a fluorescent magenta with orange shading which does not shatter (this variety travelled 200 miles by rail and road to a show and never lost a petal) Dryden, vivid scarlet with white eye, Elizabeth Bennett, a bright shocking pink with profuse flowering, Doris Moore, a glorious cherry red and Queen of Italy, a delicate pale pink on white ground.

Some doubles falter a little in a wet season, but still put up a brave show, and in one wet summer I placed the following high on the list for a most commendable display; Forest Maid, a most beautiful hybrid with soft crimson flowers of quality, Tanya Richardson, a striking red prolific and long lasting, Magnificent with masses of soft pink trusses that almost eclipse the plant, Shimmer, an irresistible apricot with white centre, Irene the first ' lady of the American geranium world ' Lorelie, the light shrimp pink with compact round trusses, and Penny, the popular neon pink. Mrs. A. M. Mayne stands high in the affections of English growers, but it is beaten to second place outside by Brook's Purple which has stronger stems, smaller but not such top heavy trusses, this alone, making it a far better subject for bedding, whilst retaining more or less the same shade.

Geraniums make too much vegetative growth in rich soil, so do not be generous with fertilisers or manure.

Although they will stand a certain amount of shade, it must be remembered that they are inherent lovers of light and sun, so open positions suit them best.

A dull wet season will result in leafy growth and not so many flowers, and very little can actually be done about this, but I pinch out the tops of the shoots to keep the plants bushy, and I cannot ever remember being disappointed with the display offered under the most adverse conditions.

A mistake that is made annually by the unitiated, is the premature planting out of geraniums in the garden, and this is often due to early sales in the market or shops by purveyors eager to cash in before the seasonal rush. The results are all too obvious when the plants settle in the cold earth, and are chilled by biting winds which can be very searching and ruthless in May. The leaves yellow, and the geraniums look so sad and miserable that they are an eyesore for a time. My advice is to never plant out until the first week in June, and then everything is in favour, with no set backs that could affect the whole constitution.

It is rare that geraniums are anything but pot or container grown when offered for sale, and before bedding out, they should be watered if dry, and later carefully tapped out so that the ball of compost is not broken. Put the plants about an inch deeper in the soil than the level occupied in the pot, and pack the soil firmly around the ball of roots to prevent the formation of air pockets, and to give stability to the plant. If the ground is very dry at the time of planting out, then water afterwards to settle them in. When once established the geraniums will require very little attention the rest of the season.

It always seems rather a pity to isolate geraniums individually in a garden, and if small beds and borders cannot be devoted to generous planting, then keep to group display by putting three or four plants together, either in mixed colours, or keeping to one variety, then the effect is far more imposing.

CHAPTER 8

THE AMERICAN RANGE

SUCH is the tremendous surge of popularity for American geraniums that it is really imperative to devote a chapter to them, because they often have such an immediate impact upon newcomers that it is not long before we have other enthusiastic growers joining our forces.

The forerunner quartet exported from America at a time when a real boost was needed, comprised of Irene, Penny, Cal and Genie, and these stocky, close-jointed varieties with large, unique foliage and massive trusses made an electrifying impression that resulted in wide and far reaching interest in geraniums. Gardeners everywhere who had normally spurned them, were suddenly clamouring for the fascinating Irenes, and a new era was born.

Their value as pot plants could not be over estimated – as show varieties they were impeccable, and for summer display outside they were first class. They were a sudden inspiration, and it was not long before those delectable pinks, Party Dress, Springtime and Rose Irene were with us. The orange scarlets and reds spilled a glory from America to England, and Radiant, Lollipop, Toyon, Seventeen, Apache, Jeweltone, La Jolla and Buccaneer set us aswoon with sheer delight. White Modesty swept through the trade, and we were enthralled with the spectacular Magnificent with its enormous salmon pink trusses, and sweet Lorelei with its shrimp pink, round compact heads flowering perfectly right through the winter in warmth.

But the inevitable happened. In the race to flood the ever growing demand for American geraniums, new varieties were jettisoned on the markets, but with such close similarity to existing ones that it was almost impossible to tell them apart, and it was obvious that somewhere along the line there was going to be an almighty confusion and mixup. The reds in particular were becoming so much alike that there was the greatest difficulty to name them correctly when apart from each other. Professional growers in this country were very quick to realise this, and the unanimous reaction was to eliminate many of the reds and pinks, and retain only the best and the most easily distinguishable.

Actually, unless a new introduction is really different and outstanding, it is unfair to give it a name ad lib and push it through the trade for distribution. Hybridists have got to work full out on really unusual and up to date geraniums and avoid drenching a market that is nearing saturation point.

On many of the American geraniums it is possible to produce fantastic heads of flowers, and I experimented with Flame Irene and Toyon, by planting them on from autumn struck cuttings, until they were eventually in eight-inch pots. They were allowed to become static on the loam bed of the greenhouse in the background, and it was not so long before they had attained a height of three feet, the roots having infiltrated through the drainage holes of the pots, and found a secure anchorage and nutrients in the soil. The leaves were five to six inches across, and the trusses were seven inches, perfectly formed, and so distinctive that it was automatically assumed by all who saw them, that they were a new race of geraniums! Root restriction in smaller pots standing for preference on dry staging, naturally curtails such vigorous growth, and brings the plants in line for show specimen.

The great floodtide of American geraniums is flowing strongly, and the plants have become a must in any collection. They are already strong trade leaders, and many are resistant to bad spells of weather, which makes them admirable for bedding outside in our completely unpredictable climate.

A great and commendable effort has been made by raisers to maintain a high standard of quality, and certainly concentration appears to centre around the semi-doubles and doubles in the States, because there, they appear to give a more durable performance than do the singles.

Treasure Chest and Showgirl were another two names to bear in mind for the former with an overlay of orange on the red makes it irresistible and the latter more solid, brighter, rounder and less shattering than Irene puts it well into the limelight.

CHAPTER 9

THE LURE OF THE REGALS

THE Regals, Pelargoniums, Grandifloras or Lady Washington geraniums are one and the same, and in England are used mainly as pot plants for display, and probably have a longer and more illustrious history than the zonals. It is well known that for more than 150 years there have been interested growers and raisers, and in Victorian and Edwardian days, the pelargonium was used to great advantage in conservatories, greenhouses, and for massed display on cottage windowsills indoors. There was only a short season of flowering during May and June in this country, and after that it was very spasmodic, so pelargoniums were assumed to be indoor

d possibly intolerant of weather conditions.
with the humble fuchsia as the most popu-
for house decoration, but during the last
ridists have made wonderful progress
of the regal, and with considerable
market potentialities, we now have
varieties with massive flowers, and a
blooming, and some of them are so
her conditions that they can actually
ow boxes, tubs and bedding out without
All this has greatly enhanced the
e regal and brought it well into the best
ts, especially for Mothering Sunday and
en, because of sheer beauty, and more eco-
nomical price, it threatens to oust the expensive and
more temperamental azalea. In point of fact it bears a
likeness when in full bloom to the azalea, but the range
of colour is more extensive and varied, and even
brighter.

The process of rooting pelargoniums is even easier
than the zonal, but longer, and they prefer cooler conditions. They are almost resistant to stem rot, and
certainly not so prone to disease, but where a zonal
cutting takes a fortnight to root, the regal will take
a month.

The medium for rooting can be coarse grit, vermicu-
lite, or John Innes seed compost, and although there is
a divided school of thought on this point, I prefer an
open propagating frame, as I find that closed conditions
with humid atmosphere lowers the general stamina of
the cuttings. Although bottom heat is not recommended,

especially by American growers, I find a soil temperature of about 50 degrees F. is cosy and helpful, and hastens the rooting period.

As soon as the cuttings have formed a cluster of roots,
pot into 3 or 3½ inches, using John Innes No. 1 compost,
or if preferred, a soilless compost. Some growers, due to
lack of space, retain the plants permanently in the
small pots and rely on routine feeding to sustain them
for a season, but to see the regal at its superb best,
potting on must be resorted to, and the plants progress
from 3½ to 5½ or 6 inches and then to 8 inches. Some
varieties will require pinching at the tips to induce them
to become bushy, but many of the modern types are
naturally stocky and well shaped without any tendency
to reach for the sky, so these carry on without stopping.

All regals require airy conditions, no humidity or
high temperatures, plenty of space and light. They are
best grown steadily, and that is why I prefer John
Innes composts for them. I found that soilless stimulated growth far too rapidly, and the plants made lush
leafage, becoming top heavy, especially in a combination of soilless compost and plastic pots. The whole
beauty of the pelargonium is in a thick set, bushy, short
jointed plant, encompassed with a mass of flowers.

To induce flowering for a certain time, it is wise to
withhold feeds for a month and keep on the dry side,
thus accelerating the period of reproduction. Such conditions are a natural stimulus in the life cycle of a plant,
and it hastens to flower and seed to perpetuate its kind.

Grand Slam and its sport, Lavender G. Slam are
without doubt two of the finest regals ever raised, and

their popularity remains undiminished over the years. The former is a superb bushy plant with a profusion of bright red flowers, and its sport is a most appealing lavender blue. Princess of Wales, re-discovered after a lapse of years, is very old but so beautiful, being carmine with white frilled edges. Its growth is inclined to be leggy, therefore it requires some control, and it is temperamental, some plants refusing to flower for no accountable reason. Nevertheless it is the regal for the collector, and worth having. Out of the ordinary is Black Butterfly, a very dark velvety maroon, smallish flowers and foliage, but eyecatching at any time.

For those who like sombre colours, the tremendously popular Dubonnet, deliciously wine red, and Marie Rober with large deep purple flowers head the list, and will give a magical display for a long time. They provide a good foil for more delicate shades.

American hybridists seem to have embodied just the right habit as regards growth and flowers in their varieties, and Gay Nineties is typical with its masses of large white trusses with rose markings on the upper petals, and rose veins on the lower ones.

White Sails with the huge white, lightly-feathered flowers was popular but the advent of Moon Rapture bearing a similarity, and obviously of the same group must be considered an all round improvement, and has been accepted as such.

Surely the premier English regal is Carisbrooke with its beautiful large pale pink flowers with crimson markings, but the growth is very vigorous, and unless there is strict root control, it can become overpowering. When fully matured it occupied so much room that I had to forsake it for the more compact types.

Applause from the American stables made another great conquest and the very ruffled petals, rose pink with white edges and throat built up flowers of massed and spectacular beauty. The plant is short and self-branching.

Many admirers were won by the great old Grandma Fischer which will never be completely eclipsed. The ruffled flowers are a clear salmon and prolific, and the plant very compact. It is still a leader of some merit.

Aztec made a great impact with its quite distinctive foliage with its blush to white flowers bearing rich markings on each petal. It blooms en masse and maintains a continuity of flowers, and another equally lovely variety is Strawberry Sundae with brilliant strawberry pink trusses in dazzling profusion.

It is impossible to name every catalogued regal, or to keep up to date with new introductions, but I must mention Lilac Applause with ruffled flowers of a remarkably good lilac shade, and Pink Bonanza, an unusual strawberry pink which makes the ideal pot plant.

Country Girl was one of my best sellers, and last year when the young plants were coming into full flower, it was almost impossible to meet the demand. The large pink blooms are borne on a fine shapely plant, which brings it right into the front line.

When the flush of bloom is over under glass, I put the plants outside for the summer, either keeping them in the pots and standing them in open frames, or sinking the pots in the garden until the autumn. If I just want the plants for cuttings I turn them from the pots and bed them, where they continue to flower, and at the same time make an abundance of vegetative growth. This is all removed for cuttings in the autumn and the mother plants are then destroyed.

Of course, pelargoniums can be kept in pots over a period of two or three years, and an annual top dressing given, combined with liquid feeds to retain them in good good and flourishing condition. They will commence flowering earlier in the spring than the very young plants, and give a most excellent all round show, but where space is limited they can become a burden by occupying too great an area.

CHAPTER 10

THE SCENTED GERANIUMS AND SPECIES

AT one time this was a very neglected group of the geranium family, and attractive mainly to the avid collector and the hybridist, although records show that the leaves of some of the varieties were used for medicinal purposes, for potpourri, and for the flavouring of cakes and puddings. Gardens for the blind were dotted with the more heavily scented types, and these were often planted close to the edge of the border so that movement near them drenched the immediate air with the alluring aroma.

Most of these plants actually grow faster and more vigorously in the garden during the summer than they do in pots, and attain shrub-like proportions, after which, room permitting, they can be carefully lifted and transferred to large pots or tubs and placed inside the house or greenhouse for protection throughout the winter. Unfortunately in this country, they are not hardy enough to remain outside. They are quite easy to propagate, although some of them take a long time to root like the regal pelargonium.

In America, the old fashioned rose geranium will reach a height of five to six feet outside, growing in conditions closest to its native habitat, and can actually be used for hedging. The foliage of this and the oak leaved variety is excellent for floral arrangers, bringing a combination of scent and artistry to designs.

In a previous chapter I have mentioned the temperamental but fascinating *P. Gibbosum*, and equally as intriguing is *Tetragonum* with its peculiar four sided stems with tiny leaves at the joints. The flowers have two white petals with long maroon stamens. This is a fast grower, and trained up a trellis or canes, presents a unique appearance. In a season, with generous treatment it will make a surprising amount of growth, but it should be kept under glass.

Probably the layman would find the species way out plants, and so far removed from modern geraniums, as to be of no more account than peculiar novelties.

Brutus at end of October

Marion Mason

Monica Bennett showing parent
Mrs. H. Cox colouring in early
Spring

Beltane

Harry Hieover

The Lovely Erodium

The Lovely Erodium (close
up)

Improved Ricard

Helen Bowie raised by
Monica Bennett

Mabel Grey with its large, rough indented leaves, small whitish flowers, and strong citron scent is quite irresistible and the demand always seems to exceed supply. If anything I should say that this is the most pungent, and I usually keep a plant close beside me when I am potting up in the greenhouse, so that I can catch the elusive drift of scent.

Very pretty is the dainty Fragrans with neat reiform leaves and profusion of tiny white flowers. It has a branching habit and is slightly pendulous which makes it ideal for hanging baskets. The sweet scent of spices arise from the plant when the leaves are lightly touched. Prettier is Variegated Fragrans, which has green foliage with cream markings, but bearing the same delightful habit as its parent.

I have seen some spectacular plants of Lady Plymouth and its sharp rose scent has won many admirers, and so too has the elegant *Crispum Variegatum* with grey-green and cream edged leaves and mauve flowers. This plant can be grown like a magnificent column three to four feet high if trained correctly from the start, but even as a small plant in a $3\frac{1}{2}$ inch pot it is certainly in the top ten. The colour is so bright and fresh that it makes a splendid foil for the more sombre types.

Another extremely handsome plant is *P. Tomentosum* with delicious peppermint fragrance and very soft, downy leaves with creamy markings. Easy to grow, eye catching as a specimen, this pelargonium is ego boosting to the veriest amateur.

One of my particular favourites is Rollinsons Unique

c

with a very pungent spicy scent, and pale purple flowers. In a five inch pot it makes a wonderfully appealing plant and is a fast seller.

Little Gem is a fast growing plant, covered in a profusion of small lilac flowers. The foliage is rough and sharply indented, and a good lemon aroma about it, but *Citriodorum* might force the pace with its neat lemon scented leaves and mauve flowers with purple marks on the upper petals.

Many of the scented geraniums have insignificant flowers, so it is quite a change to turn to Lothario with the bold show of scarlet bloom and dark green leaves spicily fragrant, and few could help but love *Capitatum* with the rose perfume and mauve flowers.

In the near future there is going to be an increasing interest in the scented geraniums, especially amongst the feminine sex, because potpourri is very trendy now, and it is so simple to collect all the petals of the summer flowers including the geranium, but nothing enhances the fragrance so much as the addition of the leaves from the fragrant varieties. These can be dried naturally during the summer, together with multi-coloured geranium petals, and there we have the basis for some very acceptable gifts.

CHAPTER I I

NITTANY LION AND
THE CAREFREE GERANIUMS

IT was inevitable that the time would come when a named geranium would be launched upon the market capable of reproducing its kind by seed, which would flower in the same season as sown. It was also inevitable that when such a geranium made its debut, it would be met by a certain amount of criticism and hostility, especially by the trade, insofar as it cast a shadow of possible mass production of future varieties, and a general slump in prices. Nittany Lion came from America where it has proven itself successfully by flowering generously during the summer following an early spring-sowing of the seed. The fact that there was a tremendous variance in the climate from sunny California and other parts of the States as compared with the British Isles was apparently overlooked or completely ignored, and with a blaze of publicity Nittany Lion roared its way towards garden lovers everywhere.

Sceptical, but very willing to try this geranium, I sowed the seed in early January in John Innes seed compost, and kept in a temperature of 55 degrees F. The germination was erratic as it usually is with geraniums, and as the seedlings became large enough to handle, they were put in $3\frac{1}{2}$ inch pots in John Innes

No. 1 compost. Growth was very satisfactory, and by May, I had a fine batch of young plants with healthy deeply zoned foliage, and showing great promise. One plant I retained in the greenhouse as an experiment, and the rest were bedded out in a good open position which was a positive sun trap. The plant in the greenhouse had two trusses of flowers open at the time of Southport show, and this was taken by officials of the British Pelargonium and Geranium Society to the show to prove that Nittany *did* flower in the same season. By late autumn the plants outside were just showing flower buds, and then came the flood of correspondence from various parts of the country, expressing keen disappointment. Beds of Nittany Lion had been planted and the overall results had been flowerless batches of geraniums with buds forming far too late in the season. Controversy raged between growers via the gardening press, and Nittany fell out of grace. In isolated parts of the country where climatic conditions were more favourable there had been flowering, but it was felt that neither the colour, which was much darker, nor the trusses could compare with the improved Paul Crampel.

Following the sensational and partial eclipse of Nittany, the Carefree group was launched via typical American publicity campaigns, and these were calculated to rock the very foundations of the geranium world.

High pressurised American salesmanship projected itself across the Atlantic, and it really made its impact in such wise that thousands of young Carefree plants were pushed through the wholesale markets in the early spring for growing on, and at bedding out time were offered in flower in 3½ and 5 inch pots with growth accelerated for the purpose by soilless composts, and despite mass shattering of petals, sold well on the strength of their name and novelty. True, they were graded by colour only as pink, salmon, scarlet and white, but to gardeners interested only in display, anything else beyond this was immaterial. To the unwary, some nurseries cashed in by offering well developed plants in five inch pots at ridiculously high prices. A seedling always looks lush, healthy and full of vigour in its initial stages, especially when assisted by soilless composts which is growth compelling.

I grew the full range of Carefree geraniums in every conceivable way . . . in pots, beds, tubs, troughs and boxes, but found petal shattering persistent, and although the shades were appealing, and plants really did flower in the first season, they were certainly not up to the high standard attained by the named varieties. A cheaper method of producing geraniums for bedding purposes certainly, but again, nothing to perturb the dedicated enthusiast. Interesting, too, for anyone who likes raising plants from seed and seeing results in the same season, but again, nothing to get madly excited about.

Hybridists on the whole could breathe freely again and continue their activities without any fear of their exacting work being imperilled by these impulse buying, trendy introductions that flash like meteorites across the horticultural skies, brightening for a time their path, but falling later into the abyss of obscurity.

The Carefree are raised easily by seed sown during early January in John Innes seed compost or a soilless compost. Germination is sometimes very erratic, but seedlings can be removed as soon as they are large enough to handle, and potted on just as other geraniums. They can be vegetatively reproduced equally as well.

Probably the Carefree strain acquit themselves more admirably in the sunny climate of California.

CHAPTER 12

GERANIUMS AS STANDARDS

THERE is a growing demand now for geraniums as standards to highlight the bedding displays and relieve the flatness. In the past much of this has been relegated to the fuchsia family, and the spectacular effect from standard fuchsias can readily and more showily be obtained from our geraniums because the flowers are bolder in both colour and formation.

Select strong vigorous types that make plenty of vegetative growth, and it must be remembered that it takes more than one season to achieve a good standard, and some allowance must be made for housing the plants during the winter. There are varieties which lend themselves perfectly to this form of culture, and amongst them are Tanya Richardson, a rich double red with well zoned foliage, Flame Irene with the round semi double, salmon red flowers, Pandora with massive single trusses so brightly red, Staple White flowering prolifically, Victorious the massy plant with clean strong foliage and huge flame trusses. These are but an isolated few from the many.

Choose young plants with straight main stems that are inclined to run upwards without signs of branching. I usually make my selection from amongst the late summer struck cuttings and keep them growing throughout the winter. The leaves are stripped off the stem leaving a head like a miniature ornamental tree, and from then onwards priority is given regarding treatment. As soon as the roots are well round the ball of compost, I transfer the plants from $3\frac{1}{2}$ inch pots to $5\frac{1}{2}$ inch using John Innes No. 2 compost, and as the plants grow, I tie the stem to a small split cane to keep them erect until maturity. Occasional liquid feeds are given, and on a mild day about once a fortnight in the spring I give a foliar feed which I find is very beneficial. This is applied in the evening so that the leaves have time to absorb it during the hours of darkness. Otherwise during the day, especially if the sun is out, it seems to dry up quickly.

Whenever leaves appear on the main stem I remove them, and when the plants have reached a height of

18 to 20 inches, I pinch out the tip to induce branching, and as soon as each little shoot resulting from this form of 'stopping' is about three inches long, I pinch the tips of those to effect further branching and thus build up a good shapely head.

When the plants show signs of being ready for a move, I pot them on into 8 inch pots, using John Innes No. 3 compost, and now they need space and full light to develop properly. Usually I dot them amongst the smaller plants, which gives them the head room they require without being a nuisance.

During the summer I liquid feed the standards every fortnight, and it is essential that the stem is well supported, especially when moved to summer quarters, outside. Otherwise summer gales are liable to snap them off.

They can be retained in the large pots, or transferred to tubs for positioning them on yards or patios for decorative purposes, or if needed for bedding, the pots can either be sunk in the earth which makes late autumn lifting easier, or the plants can go direct into the bed. It is just a matter of choice. Keep the main stem clear of all growth throughout the season, or the standards will revert to bushes.

Very effective displays are achieved by mass bedding of one variety of geranium with standards of the same type taking off the flatness, or a bed of variegated foliage plants look fantastic as a background for standards of a rich, glowing red. Actually there is no limit to the uses of standard geraniums.

CHAPTER 13

GERANIUMS FOR BASKETS AND WINDOW BOXES

THERE was a time when hanging baskets and window boxes were very much in vogue, used perhaps more generally in the country, and then again, on the changing wind of fashion, there seemed to be a decline in the popularity of such summer decoration. Happily there is always a welcome revival which swings the pendulum right back, and we have what is known today as a trendy line, and this gathers so much momentum that a season brings a well established foundation. This is what happened with hanging baskets.

It was realised that they could be suspended like huge flower balls to brighten the harsh contours of modern buildings . . . they could bring a real, living beauty to industrial areas, hanging in porches, doorways, in verandas, or from wrought-iron angles fixed to uninteresting walls and fences. Their uses for street decoration was legion, and many a town is now enlivened during the summer by beautiful baskets.

When it was fully appreciated that hanging baskets were to become a way of the gardener's life, plastic ones in many designs were launched upon the market, including some with attached saucers to retain the drippings after watering. They met with some opposition on the grounds that they added a certain amount

G*

of artificiality, and that wire containers with moss were more natural looking, and that plants could be pushed between the moss to make a complete ball of flowers when grown, but actually this was negated by the fact that the plants trailed over the sides of the plastic baskets, and eventually obscured them from sight. Added to this the plastic container was warmer, held moisture longer, and the plants remained in perfect growing condition right into late autumn. There was no necessity to use moss or drainage, so actually there was room for more compost which was all to the good for the plants.

The wire type are traditional and cheaper, but have to be lined with moss. To prevent undue splashing when or after watering, some polythene can be placed next to the moss with one or two small holes in the base to allow excess moisture to drain away. If this is done then it is virtually impossible to push small plants through the sides of the basket, as a filling, although when the geraniums have fully developed there are very few gaps.

If large baskets are being used, and there is some fear regarding weight for hanging, then a soilless compost should be considered, but a word of warning here, because more attention will be required as regards watering and feeding. I prefer John Innes No. 3 compost for all baskets carrying geraniums because I think that they require plenty of stability and all the natural nutrients it is possible to give the plants in such restricted room.

A well balanced basket is made up of about three ivy

leaved geraniums and one upright for the centre, but care should be taken that the very vigorous types are avoided. In fact the dwarf varieties are ideal for centre pieces.

Care should be taken also that enough space is left in the basket for watering. A mistake that so many people make is to pile the compost up so that every time water is given, it just runs off in a shower and the plants are still left high and dry.

Window boxes are a different proposition altogether, because the length and width is adjusted to the sills, but there must be a depth of at least eight inches. It is most important that if the boxes are fixed on upstairs sills they must be very securely anchored.

If wooden boxes are used, it is advisable to treat the inside with Cuprinol which, unlike Creosote, will not harm the plants at all. It is possible to have plastic window boxes now which are far more durable. Drainage holes are necessary because in a very wet season, there would probably be excess moisture which geraniums find intolerable. The plants can be put direct into compost, after being removed from the pots, or the pots could be arranged in the boxes, packed with moist peat, in which case they would respond to frequent changing if there should be any deterioration in the plants. Actually it is just a matter of personal choice whether they are treated in the manner of a plant trough, or as a summer permanency.

If plants are desired to intermingle with geraniums, then trailing lobelia, trailing nasturtiums, petunias and French marigolds are useful for building up in baskets.

Outstanding ivy-leaved geraniums for this purpose are Beatrix Cottington with large trusses of deep purple rosettes which are very durable, Blue Peter, a pale mauve-blue, Galilee, a great lasting favourite with double rose pink flowers, La France, a never failing winner with delightful light mauve flowers, delicately feathered with white and purple on the upper petals, Millfield Gem, a beautiful semi-double hybrid with off-white flowers, maroon feathered, Souvenir De Chas. Turner, very prolific with large deep pink trusses and very attractive foliage.

L'Elegante is unusually lovely with small variegated leaves that gives the plant such a close resemblance to ivy that it is often mistaken for such. Grown principally for its foliage, the flowers are quite free and pretty, being almost white with purple veining on the upper petals. If the plant is allowed to go dry, or is grown very cool, the margins of the leaves become pink which makes it considerably more appealing. In a basket I like L'Elegante on its own, and usually put three plants to a twelve inch size.

For window boxes the ivy leaved varieties can be used most effectively, but it is best to include some upright growing ones, and the coloured leaved zonals are excellent. Dwarf geraniums are often planted most attractively, and some of the shorter growing Americans look good. A mixture is more fascinating than keeping to one variety.

The ivy leaved geraniums are excellent for indoors for training up trellis screens, or trailing from shelves or brackets, but they must not be put in shade, or even partial shade. Fullest light possible when used in the house.

CHAPTER 14

WINTER FLOWERING GERANIUMS

PROBABLY it is the advent of so many other types of flowering plants giving gorgeous displays in the winter, that have more or less thrust the geranium into the background for this purpose, but personally I still think that there is plenty of scope for accepting the zonals as very much with it, where facilities provide for extension of the flowering period.

By maintaining a gentle heat throughout the winter of 45 to 50 degrees F. it is possible to have flowers throughout the twelve months, which is no mean achievement by any standards. Of course, the short days quite naturally have some effect upon the plants through lack of sufficient light, with the result that the foliage is not such a robust green, and the trusses are smaller, with some of the colours not so true, but one is compensated by the fact that the flowers last much longer with very little petal drop. As a matter of fact one truss on a new seedling of mine commenced to open in early December, and by the end of February was only just showing visible signs of deterioration, but there were two healthy buds to follow on. Actually I did wonder if it had set up some new kind of record, although I noticed that flowers on Helen Bowie and Lorelie came through their fifth week intact. The cool, dull days are not so exhausting, and do not force the pace too fast, so even though the plants are allowed to flower and slowly grow on through the winter, it does not adversely affect the constitution during the ensuing summer, and I have never noticed any lack of vitality.

To have a supply of young plants for this purpose, it is best to start in April or May by rooting cuttings, and going through the process of potting into $3\frac{1}{2}$ inch and later into $5\frac{1}{2}$ inch pots, which in most cases would be the finals. Concentrate on building up the plants ready for the winter by pinching out the tips and getting really bushy, shapely plants. The pots can be stood outside in the summer in a sheltered position, but do not let them go dry as dust in the hot spells or there is going to be loss of leaves and a series of checks. Care for these geraniums, of which so much will be expected in the dormant months. Towards the end of September, it would be wise to commence moving under glass, just in case there might be a few spiteful frosts, and give the plants as much room as possible so that they are not over crowded.

If there are some nicely shaped plants outside which were bedded for the summer, these could be carefully lifted and potted up, as they often commence a new period of flowering after the initial shock of transplanting. Towards the end of October, I give my plants a light top dressing of John Innes No. 3 compost, and once a month afterwards, on a mild day, a foliar feed.

Some geraniums refuse to offer much during the winter, but I have found the following most excellent; Tom Thumb, the prolific little dwarf with masses of tiny pink trusses, Brutus, Pandora, Victorious, Nanette, Plato, Irene, Lorelie, Staple White, Genie, Penny, Helen Bowie, Toyon, M. Koveleski and Dryden, all of which are described elsewhere. There are many others of course which would fill the role of winter flowering geraniums, and it is conceivable that in the not too distant future, hybridists will direct their attentions to the production of varieties that will give perfect trusses in the dreary months of the year.

Do not over pot any geraniums intended for winter flowering, as this will encourage them to make more vegetative growth at the cost of the bloom. Keep the roots fairly restricted because they certainly have no tendency to grow so fast at this time of the year, and are not likely to become pot bound. At any rate, they can always be repotted in the spring, and this will revitalise them.

CHAPTER 15

GERANIUM FLOWERS FOR CUTTING

ONLY in recent years has it been fully realised how valuable the flowers of the geranium are for the floral arranger. It has certainly taken the dedicated artists of this great cult to initiate a tremendous revival of many plants and flowers in their never ending quest for mediums to interpret designs, and geraniums were accepted whole heartedly because of their vast colour range.

The flowers will last a fortnight in water if cut before they are full blown. It is best to break off the stem at the joint because it comes away cleanly, and then cut off the slight bulge at the end of the stem to enable the water to be taken more freely. Sometimes it is advised to cut off the flower with scissors or secateurs, leaving a piece of the stem on the plant, but this is very untidy, and exposes it to die back and botrytis. A neat break at the joint leaves no wound or scar. Put the flowers into water immediately.

The semi-doubles and doubles are the longest lasting because the petals do not shatter so easily as the singles, yet, on the other hand, I have transported single geraniums two hundred miles by rail and scarcely lost a petal. If the plants are well grown, and the trusses strong with well developed pips, they seem more enduring, and then the singles become extremely adaptable.

A poignant arrangement I once saw which featured geraniums made me realise how many effective designs could be made with the flowers. This particular one was supposed to represent war and conflict, and consisted of an entanglement of barbed wire, a torn banner, and a drift of Irene trusses red as blood. It was beautifully created and the impact was there.

Another memorable display was of bronze beech leaves, and a gorgeous formation of many shades of red working from soft gentle colours to the boldest and most arrogant tones. It held all the beauty of summer subtly entwined with oncoming autumn.

Delightful line arrangements in varying pinks and silver foliage, and the vivid orange of Koveleski, Orange Fizz, Orangesonne and Alpine Orange blended with fiery autumnal tints of foliage have made such lasting impressions on my memory, that I am convinced geranium flowers rank high in the cut flower world.

In the winter I have found the flowers invaluable too, for wreath work, filling in lots of gaps with their brightness when other types of flowers were scarce or costly. I have many times improvised with the red doubles in place of carnations with commendable results.

Much can be done with the flowers of the regals too. I remember when I was a child, my father regularly used regals for buttonholes, and very elegant they always looked. Very dainty corsages can be made with them too, and the prettiest basket arrangements. The regals have long life in water, and will keep a surprising length of time in wet oasis.

Outstanding zonal varieties for cutting are Gillian Gifford, Barbara Bennett, Brutus, Flame Irene, Koveleski, Radiant, Francis James and Queen of Italy, because they have long stems, but again, these are but a few of many.

CHAPTER 16

FEEDING

IT is wrongly assumed by far too many small time growers that geraniums require a starvation diet to ensure maximum flowering capacity and best results, but I have yet to see evidence to support this theory. It is like expecting a starved child to grow up healthy and vigorous whilst lacking all the nutrients that go to build up a sound constitution.

True, a geranium grown poorly, will make an all out effort to perpetuate itself at the cost of vegetative development by yielding a mass of poor flowers, but the plant itself becomes deplorably exhausted, continuing to cling tenaciously but very precariously to life.

The first aim of the grower should be to produce a

good, well balanced plant, which can sustain itself through a season, carrying a continuity of first class trusses, and this can only be achieved by a reasonable approach to sound cultivation.

It is well appreciated that the geranium is one of the most adaptable and tolerant of pot plants, but the happy medium has got to be found between two major faults in the general growing process. Geraniums do not really enjoy poor, impoverished conditions inside or outside, such as is so frequently meted out to them, and neither do they give of their best in very rich soil or compost, because the tendency then is to make an abundance of leaf and stem, so between these two extremes we find the foundation for giving just what the plants require to bring them to peak condition, and that should be the constant aim of every grower, whether amateur or professional. If a plant is worth growing, it is worth growing well, and this is a sound policy to adopt in the world of horticulture.

If the plants are growing in pots in a soilless compost, there very soon comes a time when supplementary feeding must be resorted to, as apart from the normal intake of the nutrients by the roots, a certain amount is leached by watering, and peat is not so retentive as loam in this respect. After seven weeks, precision feeding is the rule and for the novice, the most simplified form of applying this is by using proprietary feeds like Bio Fluid, Liquinure, Marinure or Maxicrop and such like, because they are practically infallible and very effective.

If straight fertilisers are used there is always the risk

that some latent deficiency will occur, and balance will be upset. For example sometimes with soilless composts, plants can develop boron deficiency which must be corrected, and such adjustment of trace elements are not so necessary when feeds embracing these essentials are given.

Should success depend on the quantity of manures and fertilisers that a grower possessed, then the one with the largest quantity would be the best cultivator, but it is the skill with which feeds are applied that pave the way to high standards in plant perfection.

Young geraniums in a good compost do not require feeds in their early life, unless through force of circumstances they are condemned to spend full time in small pots, in which case it will be essential to feed to afford them sufficient stimulants to carry on normally. I commence to feed pot grown geraniums under glass in June when most of them are in 5 inch pots, and this is given once a fortnight if they are in John Innes compost, but only where plants appear to be hanging fire for sustenance. If they are growing steadily with good colour, I go three weeks.

I have great faith in foliar feeding, and have derived tremendous benefit by using Murphy's FF. Also I tested out the Poliverdol aerosol on some very cherished eight-year-old plants of Monica Bennett which were the originals of my stock. The foliage was getting smaller and smaller as was to be expected on plants of that age, but the improvement after a few foliar feeds was so obvious that I became dedicated to this form of feeding. Starting at the end of January under glass, I chose mild, frostless evenings just before darkness fell, and sprayed the plants once every three weeks. This seemed to be the best way because the moisture did not dry off too quickly, and the leaves had a chance to absorb it thoroughly. During the summer when the plants were in full flower I ceased spraying to avoid the possibility of causing damage to the petals.

Once a month all the plants are given a dose of magnesium sulphate (Epsom Salts), which helps to intensify the colour of foliage and flowers. It can be applied by sprinkling evenly round the surface of the pot, about a teaspoonful, and watered in, or an ounce of the salts can be diluted in a gallon of water and the plants watered liberally. If magnesium is present in the compost, it can do no harm by adding more.

On variegated leaved varieties like Mrs. H. Cox, Burdett Coutts and Dolly Varden do not over feed because you may destroy the brilliance of the colour combination in the structure of the foliage. This is very apparent when comparison is made between plants bedded out in normal garden soil when the colour is at its most intense, and plants nurtured under glass and given too rich a living.

In early January I give all the established plants a dose of Sequestrene which corrects chlorosis, often present through lack of light and sun at this time of the year, and it contributes largely to restoring some vigour in plants that are not doing too well. The sequestrene is long lasting, and yet quite readily available to subjects treated, therefore its dual purpose cannot but be beneficial.

For pot plants generally it is advised that 1 to 3 teaspoonfuls to 3 pints of water and apply the liquid as normal watering. For the geraniums I put one heaped teaspoon to the three pints of water, and find it a splendid stimulant.

It is natural for geraniums to lose a lot of colour during the dormant months, but by care and attention in the right direction, avoiding neglect, and giving as much treatment as one would during the summer the plants can maintain themselves in excellent condition.

Surprisingly enough a number of growers think that a sprinkling of bone meal on the surface of the pots is going to give the desired results to geraniums, but whilst it is first class for a long term policy in the open ground, it is not suitable for pots because bonemeal is slow in action and active for at least four years. Nothing can better liquid feeding due to its immediate availability to the plants, and easy assimilation by the roots.

CHAPTER 17

EXHIBITING

To the raw recruit, showtime seems very remote, and an almost unattainable status to reach, although in actual fact it should be the beginning and the end, and the never failing source of inspiration for anyone interested in growing.

Shows are the shop window of horticulture, presenting the ultimate in perfectionist culture, and if they can continue to infuse even a glimmer of competitive spirit in the ordinary gardener, then they will merit their existence.

Everyone who begins to grow a specialist subject like the geranium, soon develops the admirable complex of trying to do that much better than his neighbour, and this is the start of the spirit that is going to create whole hearted interest in his hobby.

Shows are the goals for which growers aim, sometimes directly and with keen determination, sometimes almost reluctantly, sometimes irresistibly.

There, the standard is set, and the invitation wide open for any improvements. Competition is the constant spur on the road to true perfection in the horticultural world, and victory is sweet indeed. Whilst the victor triumphs in his well earned gains, the loser should by no means be discouraged. Indeed, his failures should be a source of inspiration to do better the next year, and the more difficult the going, the greater the sense of satisfaction in scoring off the prizes

Whilst the monetary gain is very useful to some exhibitors to offset costs of showing, it should not by any means be the primary stimulus to showing. Sportsmanship comes very strongly into the theme of things here, and must be the sound foundation on which any successful society is built. Internal dissension between exhibitors, jealousies, animosity towards judges, lack of co-operation between members and officials is all going to eventually undermine the whole constitution of a society.

When a grower becomes keenly interested in a specialist subject, it is advisable to join a good local society, and a national one, and upon his entry as a member, he meets the people that matter most in his hobbyist world, makes new friends, gains experience, and becomes an exhibitor, but his approach towards the society must be one of strong comradeship . . . a preparedness to make and keep friends.

Judges must not be regarded in a defeatist atmosphere, and it is the honest duty of the society officials in all fairness to the exhibitors to see that only qualified judges are engaged, who are conversant with every peculiarity and individuality of the plants concerned. I really think that the days are fast declining when judges were extremely biased, and to a great extent motivated by their whims and fancies in relation to varieties.

The majority of judges now are first class growers, with a deep understanding of their subject. No glimmer of bias should creep in regarding colour or variety, and all exhibits should be considered from a high standard of supreme quality, and in sparse classes where quality is obviously low, prizes should not be awarded even at the cost of encouraging exhibitors, because automatically it is lowering the standard of the show.

If exhibitors realise that their judges are going to

uphold and adhere to these standards, they have something to really fight for, and there will be no intense
dissatisfaction and mistrust. I would like to stress how
very important it is that when results are known and
discussed, there should be no aggression between victors
and losers. The true show spirit is where the loser can
walk up to the winner and offer sincere congratulations.
If an exhibitor feels justified in making a reasonable
complaint, then seek out the judges and quietly reason
why. An answer can usually be found and problems
resolved.

The salient points to strive for in growing plants for
show is to make sure that they are neither over, nor
under potted. The plants have to be shapely, and this
is attained by a series of ' stops ' which induces branching. For example, aiming at a June show, I select
autumn struck plants, and the first pinch comes at the
end of October. I keep the geraniums in gentle heat
(45 to 50 degrees F.) during the winter to encourage a
steady growth, and as soon as the shoots are about 3
to 4 inches long, I pinch the tips out again. At least
seven to eight weeks before the show date I cease
' stopping ' and allow the plants to concentrate on bud
development.

The trusses should be evenly spaced to give balance,
and on the show date must be well formed, full, brightly
fresh with untarnished petals, with maximum size
for the variety and thus could well collect 20 clear
points.

In assessing the merits of the truss, the pips or individual flowers must be closely scrutinised and petal

formation is taken into account. Collectively the umbel or truss may look first class, but singly the pips could fall short.

Foliage is an indication of the health and vitality of the plant, and with the scented leaf group, strength of scent peculiar to that variety is as important as the general condition of the plant.

In the variegated geraniums where they are normally rich and vivid, there should be no subdued shades, and zoned leaves should be clearly defined. No suffusion should spoil the butterfly markings on Happy Thought and its progeny, and any foliage on modern varieties which is comparatively zoneless, should be fresh and vitally alive looking.

General presentation on the show bench counts too. Nothing is so distracting and objectionable as dirty pots, and in the past when so many clay ones were in use, they were usually concealed by moss or bark, or even fern, but now with the advent of plastic pots there is no possible excuse.

According to B.P. & G.S. standards set up officially to stabilise rules for showing, miniatures are considered to be normally less than 5 inches from soil level to top of foliage, and the head should be carried above the leaves on a stem not longer than 5 inches, and leaves should not exceed $3\frac{1}{2}$ inches across.

Dwarfs are normally more than 5 inches but less than 8 inches from soil level to top of foliage, and the trusses should be borne on stems not longer than 8 inches. Leaves are not limited in size, neither are the flower heads.

A standard should be 28 inches to the first break, and a half standard 20 inches, and the plants should be full of buds and flowers.

Ivy leaved geraniums can be tabled in many attractive ways, either in baskets, pots, or trained over wire cages, but in each case the maximum beauty of the plants must be emphasised, with abundance of bloom, good foliage and complete density of form.

Regals should be encompassed with flower, and the heads should not be too small or thin for the variety. They are better if slightly dome shaped to extract the greatest sphere of beauty, with clean foliage and freedom from white fly, which so often makes the pelargonium a host plant .

The flowers must be fresh and untarnished, and of good colour.

Transport over a distance to shows, can be a major problem, especially as regards single varieties and regals, but I have found that long car journeys in summer when it is difficult to control heat inside the vehicle, and the unavoidable bumping at times over rough roads can involve a great amount of shattering of trusses, whilst transport by passenger train in the parcel van will ensure almost perfect arrival.

I use a light plywood box about a yard long, 18 inches deep and 2 feet wide with strong handles each end. Slots at each corner allow a curved strip of alloy to slip in firmly to form a frame 2 feet high from the top of the box, over which a sheet of clear polythene is secured to prevent draughts or rain damage to the flowers. In this way the plants will travel 100 miles, as they did last year without losing more than two or three petals.

This seemed to me to be the perfect cheap medium for conveying plants in $3\frac{1}{2}$, $5\frac{1}{2}$ and 6 inch pots. Extremely expert with the conveyance of immense plants in large pots over a far greater distance, is Iris Munro, the Scottish champion from Inverness, Scotland, and again, she travels with the geraniums by rail, and these are packed in wooden crates, arriving in good enough condition to sweep the board, and collect the major portion of the prizes and cups.

I saw two examples of plants that had travelled by car to the show in June . . . the regals had lost most of their flowers, and a batch of miniature singles were flowerless, which is a real heartbreak for exhibitors who go to the expense and trouble of entering shows.

It is advisable to water the plants well before staging, so that during the long period on the show table they remain in fresh condition. Fortunately geraniums are extremely tolerant plants and stand show environment really well.

CHAPTER 18

WINTER CARE OF GERANIUMS AND PELARGONIUMS

In all probability it is the winter period which spells disaster with so many geranium growers who do not possess the immediate facilities to carry their plants through the slow dormant months when light and heat is at the minimum.

First there is the eager amateur with no greenhouse, who, of necessity, must take his stock into the house if his enthusiasm spurs him on to this effort despite possible intervention from the housewife. Conditions under these circumstances are more artificial to the plants, and there will be a strong tendency for them to become leggy and pallid as the weeks go by, but at least they will survive and be capable of yielding cuttings for the spring. They can be kept in pots or boxes in a position as light as possible, being taken inside about mid-October providing the frosts have been held at bay by a good autumn. Otherwise it might be wise to house at the end of September. It is all a matter of watching the weather as regards frosts. Water only sufficiently to prevent the pots going dust dry . . . in fact as long as the plants are kept alive and moderately healthy, then you need not fear.

Another alternative is to take a long term risk of uprooting your plants at the end of the season, shaking the soil off the roots, tying them in a bundle and hanging them upside down in a frost proof shed. This is an old-fashioned method and could incur substantial losses, but a few might be salvaged. In the spring they are potted up again and lightly trimmed, watered, and then follows the waiting to assess the casualties.

A better way to try and preserve a stock I think, is to take cuttings in August when air and soil is still warm, and these can be rooted quite easily outside in the garden, even if they are broken off and just inserted in the soil alongside the parent plant. When rooted, and this will be apparent from the fresh, growing look about the cutting, the young plant should be carefully lifted, and either potted or boxed up to be taken into the house. Such young plants will winter quite well and continue to make some slow growth if given some care and attention during the winter. Undoubtedly they will become leggy and drawn through lack of full light, but the tops can always be removed in the spring and used for cuttings, while the 'pinching' will induce branching of the plants.

For the grower with a small greenhouse, this can present problems unless there is some form of heating during the very cold spells. Because of the area of glass, frost penetration can be deadly if the house remains cold, and the whole crop of plants will perish, so even paraffin heating is better than nothing. Mind you, there are some very excellent heaters on the market today, but there are times when insidious fumes escape into the air, probably undetected by a human because they are so fractional, but the result will be seen in the crinkling of the foliage, and sometimes a breakdown of the tissues which shows as browning or drying of the leaves, often mistaken by the amateur for disease. Fortunately this rights itself as the need for heating declines and the spring advances.

Sheets of polythene lining the greenhouse will conserve heat and boosts the temperature up as much as ten degrees, but I noticed that there was a far greater susceptibility to damping and botrytis amongst plants, than in a greenhouse where there was plenty of air movement and light. Also there was quite a lot of moisture dripping and heavy condensation which is at variance to the geranium's requirements.

A temperature of 45 degrees F. is plenty for the geranium family and I like my plants standing on the wooden slat staging where watering is easily controlled, every pot is quickly eyeable, and dead flowers and leaves removed without difficulty. As a matter of fact all the plants should be checked over each week and cleaned up, because it is a perfectly natural process that in the winter they lose some leaves, and apart from giving an untidy appearance, they will be sources of disease unless taken away. During the tenure of dormant months, the pots may be packed together fairly close because very little growth is made, but with the advent of February and the lengthening of the days, forethought must be given to the normal expansion of the plants and they will have to be spaced out better so that development will not be too restricted.

Where heat is available, it will be possible to commence taking cuttings soon after Christmas, and as fast as these root and are potted up, they act as replacements, and in their young state, demanding less space, could result in the clearance of the parent plants altogether.

From late October until February, water very sparingly, waiting until the plants are showing signs of drying out, then fill the pots. I believe in applying water only when the plants require it, and then giving generously, not teasingly. Frequent slight watering is not going to help at all, and always remember that he who masters the art of the watering can, has reached the status of a good gardener.

In some areas tap water is very hard and not really good for a number of pot plants. We have some rain water tanks, but where water has to be hosed from the tap, we store it for a few days in tanks and then use it. I do not find it essential to take the chill off even in the winter, for I believe the tougher you can grow geraniums the better.

I do avoid applying moisture on frosty and foggy days, for it only aggravates the conditions under glass even though there is some heat. Far better to allow the plants to go really dry.

Maxim Koveleski

Mary Screen 1972
introduction

Young Standard Chang

Pelargonium Paul
Crampel

Pelargonium Willi
Knolle. Fuchsine pink;
slight white eye, deeper
feathered marks on upper
petals; dwarf habit.

Regal pelargonium Ri-etha

Brutus in winter

A Humex heated frame showing the soil warming cables (normally covered with earth)

Greenhouse staging with PVC mesh top

CHAPTER 19

PESTS AND THEIR CONTROL

FROM my personal experience in growing a wide range of plants, I would say that the geranium family is far less troubled by pest than most groups, and if the policy of prevention is better than cure is adopted throughout, then the risk of any infestation is remote indeed. Hygiene under glass is of major importance at all times, and if pests are to be controlled, then the breeding grounds for them must be eliminated.

At least once a year give the greenhouse a thorough clean out, and if not repainted, then a wash down with a solution of Jeys Fluid works wonders. If there is any brickwork upon which the silling rests, then whitewash that, and any accumulation of old pots, paper and rubbish beneath the staging should be removed and destroyed. Leave no deposit of dead flowers and foliage on the floor, and keep a bucket or box handy for dropping litter in.

The horticultural market today, caters completely for the eradication of pests, so if you are unfortunate enough to be troubled with an invasion, do not despair for there are means of control which are quite safe in the hands of the merest novice.

I find that if routine fumigation is carried out, one is practically trouble free, although it must be remembered that pests, especially the aphis, can build up

D

an immunity to one type of spray or smoke, so it is best to vary occasionally. Topglass Smokes are excellent, and simple to use being in cone form, and I alternate with Darlington Auto shreds which are harmless to all plants. Then there are Fumite smokes and other good brands. I prefer smokes because in a greenhouse there is complete envelopment of the plants, whereas if spraying is adopted, it is often a case of hit and miss.

Spraying the underside of leaves

Probably the most common, yet the most simple to combat is the greenfly. It is a prolific breeder and sap sucking, therefore can be the means of spreading virus diseases. It causes distortion of the young growth, and unsightly marking on the leaves which is sometimes never completely eradicated. A preference is shown for the scented leaved varieties.

To me, White Fly has always assumed the proportions

of the really deadly pest, probably because I remember as a child, my father forbidding entry to his greenhouses by anyone who owned a small house infested by this fly. He used to maintain that it could be conveyed even on one's clothing, and its presence was so insidious and persistent that stringent measures were adopted to prevent any possible infiltration into the houses. The early presence goes unnoticed, and as White Fly cluster in colonies on the undersides of the foliage it is often difficult to detect, therefore breeding goes on peacefully. Signs are later seen when a plant is touched and some of the fly take wing like little white spots, or on a warm day, some of them may be observed flying from plant to plant. The answer is immediate action, and it is best to use smokes which are efficient in dealing with this particular pest. Repeat the fumigation three or four times giving ten day intervals, so that the fly hatching out of eggs are destroyed.

White fly has a strong preference for Regal pelargoniums, and that is why some people will not grow them, but I think it is foolish to bypass such a lovely plant when control and precaution is in the hands of the grower.

Sometimes Red Spider is a nuisance where Ivy Leaf geraniums are grown, but it is comparatively rare except in houses that are not kept very clean. The spider is extremely minute, and often is only detected in advanced stages when a rust like residue appears on the undersides of the leaves, and they commence to yellow and look sickly. Red Spider revels in dry, hot conditions, but where there is plenty of humidity and moisture, an

Typical caterpillar damage

attack is negligible. Spraying can be adopted, but under glass it is best to use a smoke specially for Red Spider, because this pest is unaffected by some fumigants.

In the summer caterpillars can create quite a trouble, and seriously damage the foliage beyond recovery. As they are voracious feeders and usually work by night on their course of devastation, it is often difficult to find their places of concealment, but I have found that where routine fumigation is practised throughout the season, attacks are very isolated indeed, and butterflies and moths are more reluctant to visit geraniums under glass, if there are plenty of counter attractions outside in the form of flowering plants and trees.

I was once asked why my flowers remained in such perfect condition for such a long period in the green-houses, and I think that part of the answer lies in the fact that we are comparatively free of visitations by flies or bees due to fumigation. It is a known fact that if flowers are unpollinated they retain their petals much longer.

With the range of pests very limited as regards regal and zonal geraniums, the next step is to examine disease and disorders which arise periodically, and probably the most dreaded because of its unknown potency is Virus, for which there is no known cure as yet. In the early spring it seems to make itself more apparent, but at the same time can be confused with other lesser troubles which might arise at that time of the year through temperature fluctuations and fumes from oil heaters.

Virus reveals itself in the spotting of foliage and distortion of foliage in the more advanced stages, and is conveyed through the sap. It is insidious because during the summer when vegetative growth is strong and vigorous, the earlier symptoms are often masked so well that it is difficult to detect, but I have seen quantities of plants floated into the markets in the spring rush, all bearing traces of virus which is still unknown to many of the amateur gardeners buying for display. The trouble is that so often new stock is propagated from these infected plants with the end product being a continuation of the spread of the disease. Control is by destruction of plants with virus, strict hygiene, and good methods of pest elimination.

Probably the most common disorder especially troublesome to the novice is Black Leg which is purely a fungal disorder. Every geranium grower experiences this at some stage, and it is invariably ignored in the trade because it does not present any major problems which cannot be righted by adjusting conditions. It spreads rapidly with blackening of the stem from the base, and it is usually cuttings which are affected during the process of rooting. The cause is often debatable because one school of thought suggests that Black Leg arises from dryness and lack of humidity, but from my own personal experiments in this direction I have found that there was a higher percentage amongst lush young cuttings given too much water and humidity. It can occur on matured plants where cuttings have been removed, but this also seems to be prevalent in late autumn and winter when temperatures are much lower and air conditions generally damp. It is rare that I have seen it happen during the summer. Also, over-watering of plants can result in Black Leg developing at soil level with the ultimate death of the geraniums.

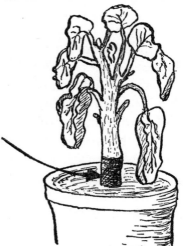

Black leg (arrow shows usual area of attack)

In the early spring some of the plants may look a little pale, usually when they have been in the pots for a length of time, and this can be due to cold wet compost, or impoverishment. I find foliar sprays of Murphy's FF or Maxicrop excellent for giving the plants a good uplift at a time when they are struggling to make some headway, but I avoid undertaking this process during frosty weather, when some damage might occur to the leaves.

Rust at one time was so remote to the British grower as to be practically negative, although in the States and Australia it was being treated more from a nuisance

Geranium rust

angle despite the fact that to the critical eye it can be quite disfiguring. Then suddenly there was an infiltration into Britain, sufficient to arouse a nagging fear especially to large growers. It was a spectre that had in a way been dreaded, and perhaps anticipated, but its eventual appearance was enough to act as a warning in no uncertain terms, and steps to eradicate it before it assumed catastrophic proportions were taken by all conscientious growers. Rust in chrysanthemums some years ago was a veritable bogey, but plant hygiene and a sensible approach to the trouble soon contributed to a major elimination, so that it became more or less a side issue to be met optimistically and suppressed by scientific aids of today.

Rust in geraniums could well be stringently controlled if there was complete co-operation amongst growers with a concentration towards this end. Regular inspection of the plants at least once a week or ten days would ensure that there were no measurable developments. Removal and destruction of any affected leaves, and occasional spraying of the undersides with Dithane is a good preventative. I have also used Hexyl Plus and found that very beneficial. The main problem is that if amateur growers are going to be neglectful or careless, they will be the means of a disastrous spread of rust by distributing affected plants amongst friends and acquaintances. Professionals are capable, or should be, of containing and preventing the disease in stock, and as most nurserymen highly value their reputation in modern fierce competition, they are prepared to do just this.

Independent of any disease, but worrying none the less, are leaf markings in the form of pallid spots which can be attributed to the effect of bright sunlight through the glass on moist foliage, and this is easily distinguished because there is no material damage of the tissues.

During the winter and early spring when oil heaters are in use, it is possible to get quite a lot of leaf distortion which one might well assume is some form of virus, but actually it is caused by fumes, and will eventually right itself when growing conditions improve and artificial heating is not so essential.

Reddening around the margin of leaves, and some varieties are very susceptible to this, is caused in winter and spring by very low temperatures, but again this is only temporary and no cause for alarm.

Botrytis will become prevalent especially where adequate heat is not available, and cause a lot of superficial trouble, particularly as the spores are air and water borne in cold, damp conditions. It attacks, foliage, flowers and stems with increasing rapidity, but as soon as there is some warmth, the disease is arrested, providing that all affected leaves and flowers are removed and burnt. A dusting with flowers of sulphur on the ends of stems which show signs of trouble will help, and smoke cones for mildew and botrytis dry up the parts.

Sometimes there is a marginal drying of the leaves, and this is invariably due to a deficiency of nitrogen, but if a well balanced fertiliser has been used for feeding, and the compost is good, it is unlikely that this trouble will occur. It is a problem associated with starved and impoverished plants.

D*

CHAPTER 20

HYBRIDISING

POSSIBLY at some time, every specialist and amateur grower will have the urge to hybridise, or produce new varieties from seed, because of the great and varied interest in this exciting process. To actually create and perfect a new strain is a tremendous thrill as I can personally testify, and I still vividly remember the impetus and driving ambition that my first medal winning geranium gave to me, and brought about a complete involvement with the art of hybridising.

Many amateurs are quite happy to purchase packets of seed and take pot luck with them, and some are happy collecting seed from plants which have had visitations from insects, and the mere fact that they can grow geraniums from such a start is a completeness in itself, because in their eyes every one is a potential winner. If this were so, the geranium world would be swamped, and a lot of the thrill of hybridising would be lost. I am not going to state emphatically that it is impossible to obtain a really worth while variety from such means . . . in fact there is always the glorious uncertainty that something quite distinctive might turn up, but on the whole, the finest introductions are acquired by careful and skilled hybridising by the dedicated people of the cult. By advanced breeding one can bring about great improvements in the whole constitution of the group, eliminating any weaknesses or peculiarities in many cases, and increasing the whole vigour of the strain. It is often wise to avoid inbreeding because as with animals or people this can often lead to an inevitable breakdown, or inherent weaknesses becoming intensified later on in the life of the plant.

To put the matter quite simply, the geranium has protandrous flowers and in such a case the stamens develop first, and the pollen sacs ripen before the stigma is matured, with the result that unless insects create a deposit of pollen on the stigma when ready, there is just a barren result. On the other hand, pollination by hand is very uncomplicated, and easier with the geranium than many other flowers.

One might well assume that all the necessities now lie in the choice of crosses to effect a world beater, but it is not so. The seedlings might bear so close a resemblance to the parents, or even revert to the original line of ancestry, that they are worthless. That is why hybridists have to destroy such a large percentage of strong young seedlings ruthlessly. At one time they were despatched to the markets as un-named seedlings to serve the purpose of bedding, but this so confused the world of geraniums that all reputable raisers destroy worthless ones immediately. Gardens used to purchase them, and if one had impulse appeal, it was given an unauthorised name, distributed via cuttings amongst friends and acquaintances with the result that strange, unknown names were constantly popping up.

Some seedlings might inherit faults from the parents

which make them undesirable, so that everything depends on the standards which the hybridist sets for himself, and these should indeed be of the highest status.

I find that June, July and August are the best times for pollinating, and having carefully selected the parents, I cover the female flowers with a bag, because it is receptive in advance. Actually I have little to fear from the visitation of insects because my fumigating programme is so thorough under glass.

It is possible that even the amateur grower has noticed many times that plants which have gone rather dry, or have been neglected a little, seem to set seeds quickly and easily under natural conditions. So being a great believer in working close to nature, I allow my plants to go on the dry side at the period of fertilising. It is very useful to have a small magnifying glass handy, and when the male sacs are ripe and the pollen is ready for use, take away the bags from the mother flowers, and with a fine camel hair brush gently remove the pollen and transfer it to the stigma. I complete this operation mid-morning, and recover the female flower for a day or two. Providing that fertilisation has not been abortive, it will soon be seen that with petal fall, small seeds are forming. Warm, sunny days will soon hasten the ripening period, and then the seed must be watched daily because as soon as the little hairy tail like a minute dandelion seed has formed at the end of the actual seed, it will be ejected from the parent and probably lost.

Some growers remove the seed and store them for a

Geranium seeds

time, but as I take them from the plant I sow them in pots, inserting a sizeable label bearing full particulars of the cross and date. Medium used for sowing can be John Innes No. 1, or seedling compost, or Levington if a soilless one is preferred. Germination is erratic, so it is best to take out the seedlings as soon as they are large enough to handle and pot them individually in 3 inch pots in seedling compost. I have known some seeds take as long as two or even three months to germinate, so do not be hasty. In fact one of the virtues that a hybridist must develop is unending patience. I allow two years before I feel that the qualities of a new variety can be safely assessed, so it is best to study the unhurried pattern of nature and work accordingly. It is essential to be able to maintain a gentle heat in the greenhouse during the winter to keep the seedlings growing, and care must be taken with watering. If too much moisture is applied the little stems will rot and that is the end of all efforts. Whilst I would not attempt to force the pace with artificial feeding, it is unwise to bring the plants to near starvation to induce early flowering. Again there are varying schools of thought about this, but to my way of thinking, unless the seedling is treated kindly and sensibly to maintain good strong growth without being lush, it is impossible to produce the maximum capabilities of the plant. There is no set time for the repotting process at all, for this can go on all the year round, so as soon as the first pots are full of root, I move the seedlings on into 5 inch size in John Innes No. 2 compost, giving the plants plenty of air and light for normal development. They are examined minutely every week, and notes are taken regarding growth, foliage and general behaviour and tendencies, so that by the time the seedlings are ready to flower, it only remains to assess the first qualities.

It would be unwise to condemn any plant on the first flower, but a very good idea can be formed as to its potentialities. If it runs too close to parents in colour and form, then it is best scrapped, but any that show promise should be set aside and cuttings taken. These can be rooted and potted on, growing them on to exhibition standards. By this, I mean that their cultivation should not be slap-happy, but determined and thorough, using a good compost, and treating the plants as if they were destined for great things. In the young stages I apply the foliar feeds occasionally, and pinch out the shoots to shape up the plants, and by the time they come into the full flush of flowering it is possible then to give a critical judgement, because they should be giving optimum results.

I do not isolate my seedlings unto themselves, because I think it is best that they accept the same conditions and environment as the established varieties, and test their worthiness accordingly.

In the third year it is possible to have made a definite selection if there are any outstanding seedlings, and grown some young plants to perfection. For the professional, the path then leads to London to put down the plants to try for awards, to name them and get them registered with the British Pelargonium and Geranium Society.

For the amateur who does not aspire so high because it is not a livelihood, the course is to take the seedlings to a geranium specialist to see if it is worthy of a place in the world of geraniums, or retain it for personal pleasure and growing, but do not give a name and distribute amongst friends and relations as such. This will inevitably increase the confusion that already exists and which the national nomenclature committee are desperately trying to unravel for the benefit of geranium growers throughout the world.

CHAPTER 21

SPORTS AND REVERSIONS

ONE of the most fascinating things about plants is their ability to throw sports, or revert to type, and to the amateur particularly this creates a tremendous amount of excitement, and often leads him to think that he probably has the most remarkable plant ever.

The point is that it is often difficult to determine which is a sport and which a reversion, and often the back history of the variety has to be traced. I myself had a typical example of reversion a few years ago before my knowledge of geraniums was so extensive as today, and it is an experience that I shall never forget.

I purchased Francis James amongst new varieties for stock, and never having seen this particular plant, grew it on to perfection and it produced fine red trusses. Then one stem produced the actual gorgeous flowers of Francis James, which I thought was a sensational sport, and I actually took this as such to London the following year, and was shattered to find it exhibited on trade stands. What had happened, I had bought a young plant of Francis James, but the cutting had obviously been a reversion, which in turn sported again and produced the true Francis James. I am afraid that I shall never live that one down!

Sports are caused by a radical change in the cells of the plants either through checks, induced mutations, the effect of some chemicals or even quite naturally, and a plant will bear a stem carrying different leaves or flowers. Sometimes the foliage is similar to the parent, but the trusses are completely different in shade, or the leaves can be different and the flowers alike. A classic example of an outstanding sport which took the Silver Medal in London in 1963 is my namesake, Monica Bennett. The parent of this great dwarf with the very dark leaves and profuse mauve-pink flowers, was Mrs. Henry Cox, the gorgeous tri-colour, and it was so extremely different that the origin was doubted, but early in the spring, Monica Bennett shows unmistakable signs of the Cox colouring on some of the leaves, which fades as the season advances.

Geraniums are not so free with sporting as chrysanthemums, but some varieties are more prone to it than others.

Two typical examples of reversion are found in Crocodile and L'Elegante. If they are treated too kindly and generously as regards feeds, Crocodile will lose a lot of its splendid variegation, and L'Elegante will throw a number of uninteresting green branches which have to be removed because they completely spoil the appearance of the plant. This reversion can be quite persistent, and it appears frequently with the silver leaved Caroline Schmidt, in the form of strong shoots with green lightly zoned leaves, which if left on the plant, would completely dominate.

Shoots, therefore, which are reversions are useless, and should be removed, but sports, which are quite different from the mother plants, and show promise, should be propagated just in case there happens to be something worth while.

Allow the sport stem to develop well, and then take a cutting from the tip and insert it in rooting medium. Mark the branch which has sported with a label, and gradually cut back some of the parent plant to enable this stem to make headway. Following the removal of the terminal cutting, side shoots will commence to grow, and these in turn can be taken. By this means it will be possible to build up a small stock. New sports can be quite as valuable as seedlings if they are distinctive enough.

Unless one is very familiar with all types and conditions of geraniums and has a fair knowledge of the ancestry of varieties, there is a continuing problem of which is sport and which reversion, but that is one of the glorious uncertainties of nature which makes it all so interesting and sustaining.

CHAPTER 22

GERANIUMS OF MERIT FOR AMATEUR AND EXHIBITOR

Unless compiling a check list, it is impossible in a book of this description to mention all varieties grown and it is inevitable that some excellent ones will be excluded, but an effort has been made to confine to geraniums that are readily available if required.

The whites are limited in their acceptance by the general gardening fraternity, because they are usually needed as a foil for stronger colours, and normally borne on the winds of fashion. At the moment, white is definitely the ' in thing '.

Winter White, Bruce, Hermine, Staple White and Cresta are worthy of special mention and should happily fulfil the needs of the most conservative growers.

Pink is always a tremendously appealing shade, particularly for women, and what finer than Pride of the West, Princess Anne, Stafford, Dot Slade, Queen of Italy, Dagata, Enchantress Fiat, Jean Oberle, Party Dress, Magnificent, Trulls Hatch and Princess Fiat, all of which bear very large trusses, and I would just have to include the exquisite Lorelie with its profusion of medium sized, round trusses.

The reds present a formidable range, from which it is indeed extremely difficult to select the best. Paul Crampel of course has always been, and always will be the most internationally known, and although it is over 60 years since its introduction, it is still a ' must ' for summer bedding schemes. It is rather a sad thing that so many inferior seedlings have been infiltrating into the markets and offered as Crampel, thus opening wide the theory that the Crampel strain had deteriorated badly with the years. Indeed, the improved Paul Crampel is so good and reliable that there is no need to wonder why it tops the pops each year.

Doris Moore is a wonderful and prolific cherry red, and the old Dryden geranium lake with large white eye remains a dazzler. Pandora with massive trusses wins a host of admirers, and so does Brutus, a vivid capsicum red with flush of orange, and pips two inches across.

The brilliant crimson-red of Showgirl, and the deeper shade of Majestic, the soft scarlet of Radiant, and the gay poppy red of Seventeen are voluptuous in their beauty. The deep orient red of Edmund Lachenal and the vivid scarlet of Jolly Roger enhance the scene, so that one wonders how it is possible to ring so many changes on one set colour.

Gentle salmon shades are more relaxing, and Susan Baldwin is a typical example of such enchantment. Cal is probably one of the purest of the salmon varieties, and Fiat is a lovely coral shade. The old King of Denmark, Marie Stalmeyer, Queen Fiat, Barbara Bennett and Genie are well worthy of mention.

Few can resist glowing orange colours, and pride of place must still go to that stalwart, Maxime Kovalevski, which, despite the fact that it was introduced in 1906, is still a very superior variety. Jane Campbell, more intense, is bewitching, and the Swiss Orangesonne is still very desired, although I think that Orange Fizz has the edge with its stronger growth, and good, bold trusses. The actual plant is far more compact too.

In the magenta range, Royal Purple and Brooks Purple are excellent doubles, and probably the best in the class for bedding as well, but some of the magentas come up with a fluorescent brilliance that is really eye catching, and outstanding for bedding purposes. Heading this list are Vera Dillon, and Plato, the latter bearing prolifically, weather resistant and keeps colour and petals well.

Amongst the picotee edged, Lady Warwick is really lovely and always in demand, but she is temperamental, and it is so difficult to build up stocks that I can foresee Susanne Screen superceding with very strong growth and huge trusses, and a deeper infusion of the red on the petal edges. Staplegrove Fancy is another delightful variety, edged and spotted variably with carmine, and quite irresistible.

Emperor Nicholas is an appealing double white edged and speckled freely with rose red, and Xenia Field still has many admirers for her white veined flowers deepening to scarlet at centre. Beltane is stronger, with a far better habit of growth than S. Fancy, and perfect round trusses of superbly formed pips. Throws abundant cuttings and beds well.

The rosebud group have a limited appeal, but finest without doubt is Dodd's Super Double which really gives a splendid display and produces very strong growth and large trusses. A lovely rose shade too.

The American Apple Blossom Rosebud is unique and very beautiful, but its growth leaves something to be desired at times. The flowers are exquisite, forming round balls, and are white edged with porcelain rose with the centre tinted lettuce green. In bloom it is quite irresistible.

Again in a limited field we find the cactus group, and probably the best known is Cannel's Firedragon introduced in 1907 and still going strong. The flowers are double signal red, profuse, gay and attractive. It makes a fine pot plant. Tangerine is pretty, a double Dutch vermilion and very colourful. Mrs. Salter Bevis is very pretty and makes a delightful pot plant with double fuchsia purple flowers, with upper petals based white.

It flowers en masse and the plant itself is compact. Well grown it is an impulse seller. As a foil to these I like the single white Snow Queen.

How very difficult it is to make a selection out of the fancy leaved group. Full honours must go to the ancient Caroline Schmidt, because the abundant large double red flowers are very fine indeed and stand out well from the silver foliage. I just cannot decide which is best out of Chelsea Gem and Mrs. Parker, and they run each other so close as to be indistinguishable at times. Both have double fuchsine pink flowers and good habit of growth.

Silver tri-coloured Dolly Varden introduced in 1880 is still a leading favourite, with signal red single flowers, not large but gay and abandoned, and temperamental Miss Burdett Coutts is adorable and worth clinging to, but lack of chlorophyll makes it a slow grower and not profuse in cuttings. It is singularly beautiful with vermilion flowers.

The bronze and gold leaved class finds us reaching out for Golden Orfe with its single empire rose flowers shading to spinel red, and I always think that His Majesty is super, especially when grown outside and the leaf colouring intensifies. The single vermilion flowers are incidental with this gem, and for bedding it has few rivals. Marechal Macmahon is another old colourful beauty, and should go on forever.

The black leaved group is a bit sombre, but no one seems able to resist the old Distinction with its wonderful pencil marking, and the happy little orient red flowers doing their best to give the plant brightness.

It is an amazing thing that leading favourites today are approaching a century in age, and still maintain an enviable dominance that can never be superceded.

Of all the butterfly leaved geraniums, the most pronounced must surely be the Happy Thought family which is really lovely, although there seems in places to be a variance in stock. A good plant should carry leaves with a bright well defined butterfly.

Crampel Master is excellent, and the vermilion flowers are large, profuse and brighter even than the Paul Crampel. Makes a superb pot plant for decorative purposes.

Supreme for all time amongst the golden tri-colours is Mrs. Henry Cox with its exquisite foliage. The porcelain rose flowers tone in very well, but I always remove them and give absolute priority to the leaves. Unfortunately, good stock of this variety is running scarce and it is advisable to take care and try to build up a stock.

Mrs. Strang sometimes known as Skies of Italy, is a faster grower with the same type of beautiful foliage, but the leaves are more serrated and not so intense, and the double flowers are Dutch vermilion.

The dwarf class is a fast developing one and new introductions seem to appear annually in force. Emma Hossler with double pink flowers and green leaves is a favourite with hybridisers, and quite pretty, and Granny Hewitt with light green, faintly zoned foliage has masses of double scarlet little flowers which gives it tremendous impact when grown at its best.

Monica Bennett with its very dark green leaves and

black zone bears a wealth of lilac single flowers that encompass the whole plant throughout the summer period, and Kelvedon Beauty, stronger, bolder, has the same appeal with deeper, more striking flowers.

Friesdorf, erratic though it can be at times is a must in any collection with its small dark zoned foliage and profusion of Delft rose, narrow petalled flowers. Lovely for bedding too on borders that are limited in space. Ideal as pot plants and gay at all times. Sometimes get a plant that grows superbly but refuses to flower.

Pretty is Opal, with dark zoned leaves and single rosine purple flowers edged with white.

Miniatures are the trend of course, and it is now impossible to bypass them because they are approaching the top of the pops with a number of growers, amateur and professional. The names are almost legion, but Bob Cratchett is good with green leaves, and single crimson flowers with large white eye. So is Dwarf Miriam Baisey with deep green foliage and single cherry flowers with white eye. Flash, a single scarlet with white throat is choice and attracts at all times. In shades of green with butterfly markings in the leaves is Red Admiral, and the double deep red flowers lends it added lustre. Flirt with dark foliage and double flowers of cream strongly flecked and streaked with pink lives up to its pert name.

Dark leaved Old Peggotty is alluring with its single velvety red trusses and dark leaves, and a fine orange trio is composed of Orange Gnome, Orion and Orange Glow, all of which make excellent pot plants.

The Vesuvius family come within the confines of

miniatures, but they will exceed the limits of height as stipulated for true miniatures when grown well and generously, and they are so easy and satisfying to the grower that they are well worth consideration when building up a collection.

A superb variety is Timothy Clifford with very dark foliage, and double porcelain rose overshot with camellia rose flowers which are carried on erect little stems throwing the trusses clear of the leaves.

The choice of regals presents a problem of magnitude, because so many are excellent, and so few poor, so it is a case of making as wide a range as possible as regards colour. Commencing then with white, Moon Rapture is fascinating with its slight veining and sizeable flowers, although Sheer Applause with its frilled edges is likely to gain more attention.

Carisbrooke, long known as 'England's best' has huge umbels of pink flowers with crimson markings, but the plant is strong and vigorous and inclined to become overpowering unless controlled.

Country Girl is a winner with large pink flowers with markings, but Aztec is showier flowering profusely with blush white petals carrying elongated suffusion of varying shades of strawberry red. Very compact and long flowering.

Nothing could ever eclipse the striking beauty of Grand Slam and Lavender Grand Slam both of which must rank as No. 1 amongst florists pot plants. It is difficult to make a decision between Solano and Grandma Fischer, for each is excellent with soft salmon flowers that encompass the short bushy plants.

Rogue, Dark Venus and Dubonnet are three excellent regals in the wine coloured shades, but might prove a little too sombre for those who like light, gay colours. They are mass bloomers, and make superb pot plants when grown to perfection, and then have so much appeal that one can overlook the brooding shade of their flowers.

I have an affection for Giant Butterfly with its lavender lower petals shading to darker on the upper ones, and plum markings. If unusual regals are desired, then Jungle Night will appeal being slightly ruffled Indian Lake, with all petals suffused and veined black, and the American Pompeii has petals almost black, but exquisitely relieved by a narrow edging of pinky white.

In the magenta group, All My Love is really outstanding because the flowers are orchid mauve on a creamy white foundation, with crimson blotches on the upper petals.

From America we again get King Midas, a well shaped plant with orange red flowers shading to apricot, profuse and never really untidy.

Royal Mascot is a delight and quite distinctive for it is a crimson velvet with a sparkling background of white, and darker radiating stripes.

From the regals we move to the indispensable ivy-leaved varieties which fulfil so many needs for the summer as regards baskets and window boxes. Foremost would be Blue Springs with excellent growth and lasting double flowers in an enchanting shade of mauve suffused with blue.

La France is supreme although it was introduced as

long ago as 1900, but its habit is perfect, and the double purple flowers have upper petals feathered white and purple. Red Galilee and Red Crousse are both fine, the former a really brilliant scarlet, and the latter a showy rose red. The rosette varieties are beautiful, and ever popular is Beatrice Cottington, a Persian rose, and Blue Peter, a pale mauve with blue suffusion. Madame Rozeine is a very soft pink and adds a variance of colour which is very acceptable when going all out for display. Pale colours never seem to get the urgent demand that richer shades do, but Double Lilac White is a lovely contrast, being pure white with the most delicate lilac veining towards the centre.

The hybrid group offer some real beauties, and Achievement is gorgeous, the semi-double rose flowers paling at the throat and flushed with pink. Millfield Gem is another well tried variety with pale rose flowers blotched and feathered with rose red, and Elsi the orange scarlet has a nice variegated leaf which is most attractive.

Scented leaved pelargoniums are the ' in thing ' now, and their popularity is on the increase at a rapid rate. This is not to be wondered at if one has caught the pine fragrance of Fragrans with its pretty little silvery green leaves and tiny white flowers borne en masse. It has a tendency to be pendulous so it is ideal for a basket.

Cedar scented Clorinda is fine insomuch that the flowers are large and a bright pink. Prince of Orange has a delicious orange aroma with small leaves and long petalled mauve flowers. Attar of Roses gives the rose fragrance, Radula the fresh lemon, and the lovely

Mabel Grey with the rough, heavily serrated leaves fills the immediate air with the scent of citronella . . . pungent, alluring and cloying.

Some of the Unique hybrid pelargoniums are well worth trying out, and I like Madame Nonin with broad curled petals that look double. The colour is neyron rose, strongly veined with turkey red. Purple Unique is very pretty with purple-mauve flowers, and a specimen plant is very handsome and colourful indeed. Crimson Unique provides a change being red and all the petals are heavily veined.

To see a well grown plant of Catford Belle in full flower is to know and love the Angel pelargoniums, and the small rough leaves and bushy habit is a foil for the flowers in two shades of purple.

Rose Bengal is also in two shades of purple but with a difference insomuch that the edges are pale. Sancho Panza and Manx Maid still retain the varying purple shades.

Here then, is a starter list for the amateur, none of the varieties mentioned so difficult that they are likely to frustrate the grower, and all of them lovely enough to arouse an enthusiasm that is likely to gather momentum each season. Once the interest is awakened and sustained, the whole cause of the geranium world will move on to greater things. New varieties will flicker across the horizon with the launching impact of modern publicity, but they will have to be good to equal the illustrious records held by so many of the very old ones which apparently show no deterioration in stock or quantity.

Once the amateur has given any of these a trial and really produced something worth while then the path lies wide open to more adventurous moves with exploratory incursions amongst the rarer types, and then the geranium fanatic will have been born.

UNUSUAL AND INTERESTING GERANIUMS

In this group we get the novelties that either have an immediate appeal, or remain gimmicky, so that the demand is never overwhelming. They are useful in building up a collection, but never reach the high light of popularity, and yet some of them are very pretty when grown as specimens.

Jeanne, or more widely known as Skelley's Pride, is attractive with deeply serrated petals, and good trusses of a rich salmon. If given generous treatment it loses a lot of its singular beauty, so I do not feed it so frequently as other types.

Actually in each class there is at least one variety which has the distinction of being a little unique in the fact that somewhere it has made a complete break away, like Mr. Wren, the zonal with flowers which have an artificial appearance. They have a splash of brilliant red on a white foundation, and although they are not borne in profusion, and the trusses are small in comparison to the plant, Mr. Wren is worth growing. Superficially it attracts, and detailed inspection only serves to reveal just how enchanting is the colouring on each flower.

New Life and Double New Life with small scarlet

and white striped petals, sometimes reverting wholly to red are fun to grow, and continue over the years to hold admirers.

Into the unusual grouping I would not hesitate to include the very controversial Stellar varieties which were introduced in Australia by Ted Both, and hit the world markets with varying impact.

All the Stellars have strange star shaped foliage, some of them quite heavily zoned, and the flowers on some are single and others double. They are not large, but in such profusion that lack of size in trusses and solidity is more than compensated for.

The lower petals are broad and serrated, and the narrow upper ones sharply forked. The plants flower quite happily through the winter in gentle heat and always look bright and gay. The white S. Arctic Star is striking, and pink S. Dawn Star, deep salmon S. Hannaford Star and the vivid S. Scarlet Gem are outstanding singles, whilst orange Ragtime, scarlet Grenadier and Pink Pixie Prince surely head the doubles. Plants grown on into larger pots have a brilliance all their own, and the flowers can be used to great effect for floral arrangements. Although unlikely to ever create a real sensation in the geranium spheres, they will possibly find a lasting niche and many admirers amongst floral art devotees.

The Birds Egg geraniums, first introduced in 1900 are delightfully distinctive and a typical example is White Birds Egg being white tinted with purple and spotted heavily on the lower petals. Single Pink Birds Egg is a lovely rose shade with white centre and the petals have rose red dots.

Coming to the miniatures and newer introductions, I was fascinated by Tweedle-Dee and Tweedle-Dum, very bushy plants with curious shiny lobed leaves with a slight fold, and large primitive flowers abundantly produced. The former is salmon and the latter a much deeper shade of salmon.

Singular too is the tiny American Variegated Kleine Leibling with minute light green leaves, white edged and crinkled, and single pink flowers with upper petals based white. A geranium for a grower with infinite patience and lack of space.

The Boar is a fascinating type, useful to hybridisers, and all purpose, insomuch that it can be trained as a climber, or planted in hanging baskets because of a pedulous habit, or it can be kept shrubby by continuous pinching back, by which means a most handsome plant can be produced. The loosely formed coral flowers are profuse, primitive in shape, and have been likened to a flight of butterflies, and this might well be so if a little imagination is used. The plant grows fast, and the cuttings root easily. The foliage is dark green with strong zoning.

Possibly Freak of Nature introduced in 1880 and belonging to the butterfly leaved group, still intrigues as much as ever it did with its variable colouring of cream and pale green, and apparent lack of chlorophyll in patches of leaf and stem. The single flowers are vermilion, and the plant is supposedly difficult, but I found that given good compost and fair treatment it was by no means temperamental, and a handsome plant was no problem to produce. It is comparatively scarce, but adds distinction to a collection.

The age old Tetragonum belonging to the 17th century has a unique fascination insomuch that the stems are all four sided with very tiny leaves, and small rose pink flowers. It is commonly known as the ' stick geranium ' and some remarkable specimen plants can be obtained by training it up cane trellising. Growth is fast so that it does not involve a period of waiting. Actually it is so unlike a geranium that few people realise that this species was one of the leading fore-runners of some of the finest geraniums in commerce today.

CHAPTER 23

DEFICIENCIES

In all spheres of plant life, deficiencies are likely to occur sooner or later, and the grower who devotes great care and interest in his plants becomes realistically aware of this, and seeks to replenish the missing nutrients, once he has diagnosed the cause and symptoms.

Geranium Enchantment held by the author in her greenhouse

Helen Bowie

The author with regal pelargonium White Sails

A general view
inside one of the
author's
greenhouses

Pinwheel flowers of
Norah Bennett

If good, well balanced composts are used and sensible methods of feeding adopted, then it is only occasionally that deficiencies might occur. In a hot season, constant watering, then it could be that iron is needed which elements, or certain environment can affect the intake of the vital nutrients required by the plant.

It is well known that all plant life needs oxygen, nitrogen, carbon, sulphur, phosphorus, lime, potash, magnesia, hydrogen and iron, and as most of these are provided naturally in the soil, it is not always necessary to add more. Magnesium is possibly the element most widely and frequently applied, and actually if this is already present, no harm can be done in adding more. It is very important to the overall development of plant life, and a classic example of its need is found where plants have been receiving normal feeding and generous treatment during the growing season, and yet have pale foliage and a general lack of rich healthy colour. Foliar spraying and root drenching can be adopted, using a mixture of 1 ounce to a gallon of water once a fortnight until normality is resumed.

If the trouble still persists, despite care also with watering, then it could be that iron is needed which supplies the chlorophyll, in which case I find that iron sequestrene supplies the answer to this deficiency. Usually lack of iron is closely allied with alkaline soils.

If plants are inclined to lose their normal compactness and develop a weaker habit of growth, or if the colour of foliage and flowers leave much to be desired, then potash will help materially by intensifying it. Also

E

it will shorten the internodes, and help to build up a much more shapely plant. Whilst potash in moderation is excellent used in this wise, if applied in excess it will completely exhaust the magnesium contents of the soil, in which case it would have to be supplemented.

This shows how careful one should be in the use of straight fertilisers. Enough is fine for the purpose to which it is applied, but over doses can upset the whole balance of nutritional structure, so that instead of helping matters, they are being further complicated.

After the long winter months when plants, through lack of light and sun have quite normally lost colour and gone pale (some varieties are more prone to this than others) I give an application of potassium nitrate (saltpetre) at the rate of one standard teaspoonful to a gallon of water, and at the same time I include one ounce of magnesium because potassium nitrate considerably depletes the magnesium contents and can create a deficiency.

It must be remembered that potassium nitrate is a powerful fertiliser which must be used most discreetly and with due respect. It should never be used as a foliar spray because it would seriously damage the leaves. Always apply as a root drench. Alternatively, a pinch of potassium nitrate can be sprinkled on the surface of the pot and watered in, but I feel that by dissolving in a gallon of water, distribution is more even and safer. The application should have a very quick effect and a noticeable improvement seen in a few days.

Geraniums on the whole are good indicator plants and speedily reflect their likes and dislikes, so that it is

usually possible to assess just what the root of any
trouble is and to apply the remedy.

CHAPTER 24

THE USES OF PELARGONIUM AND GERANIUM SOCIETIES

When one is interested in the cultivation of a
specialist plant or flower, even if the growing of such
is approached purely and simply from the amateur's
status, with no objective towards exhibiting, it is a
decided asset to join a society to meet people with the
same hobby. Also there is the continuous pooling of
constructive information and all the knowledge and
modern methods associated with producing the best
from the plants. Meetings, talks, lectures and forums
enlighten the scene.

When I first joined the British Pelargonium and
Geranium Society, branch and affiliated societies were
few and far between, and I felt that to get to know my
plants thoroughly, I must be in contact with specialists
and learn to talk their language. I never realised then
just how much pleasure and sustained interest I was
to gain, nor how many valuable friendships I should

make. On my initial visit to London, a stranger in a strange land, and a very raw recruit indeed, I found nothing but help, kindness and encouragement which closed around me with a warmth that was all enveloping. This set me on the course that was to open wide the vast and exciting world of the pelargonium. Society literature and the Year Book yielded all kinds of ideas and opinions about geraniums, and combined with progressive and personal practical experience, my knowledge and enthusiasm increased rapidly.

I joined the International Society in America, and through the medium of their journal, gained some correspondents, amateur and professional. I learnt a lot about types of greenhouses, heating and conditions in various parts of the states, and the types and varieties of geraniums and pelargoniums grown, and of the vast commercial propagation where in Southern California 110 acres of one nursery are devoted to the raising of millions of young plants. From Canada I gained very interesting information from growers who are experimenting with basement cultivation under artificial lighting, and this is being met with some measure of encouraging success, and a means of bypassing severe winters.

Now it is hoped to develop geranium and pelargonium societies in Canada to meet the growing needs of amateur gardeners.

Then I joined the South African Society, energetically run by a most dedicated group, and through the pages of their first class journals gained further information of how the plants were grown in that

climate which is the natural habitat of so many of the
intriguing species. Grown in conditions vastly different
from ours where glasshouses and close protection is not
essential, and where many pelargoniums grow wild, I
gained another absorbing insight into the life cycle of
our plant.

Friends in Malta enlivened my inexhaustible thirst
for knowledge with accounts of the uninhibited and
vigorous growth of geraniums there, and all the year
round flowering outside, some of them being used for
hedging and as climbers over walls. Still not satiated
with pelargonium news I joined the Australian Society,
and secured some engrossing friendships with lady
members, and from them I came to know about the
first geranium conservatory ever to be built in that
country. Situated in the Botanic Gardens at Geelong it
is unique insomuch that the sides are open, and the
galvanised steel purlins will support a ribbed sheeting
fibreglass roof in the shape of an octagonal pyramid.
The plants will be displayed on all round wire mesh
shelves rising in tiers, and edging the conservatory will
be borders outlined with low stone walling to hold
sufficient plants to bring the total to about 1,000. This
great venture will be another milestone for the enthusiasts of Australia.

Regals predominate in that country because apparently they give better results. All these associations
with societies around the world helped to create a
complete picture of the geranium and pelargonium, and
eventually transported me into the regions of hybridising. I still keep all my contacts and would most sin-

cerely urge all geranium growers to join some society in order to extract optimum pleasure and interest.

The address for the British Pelargonium and Geranium Society is Mr. H. Wood, Secretary, 129 Aylesford Avenue, Beckenham, Kent.

The International Society is 1413 Shoreline Drive, Santa Barbara, California 93105, America.

The South African Pelargonium and Geranium Society, P.O. Box 8574, Johannesburg, Republic of South Africa.

The Commonwealth Pelargonium and Geranium Society, 1449 Ferntree Gully Road, Scoresby, Victoria 3179, Australia.

A LIST OF GERANIUMS

RAISED AND INTRODUCED BY THE AUTHOR

Iris Munro. An outstanding zonal with strong line of American blood. Strong plants, heavy foliage. Large compact double trusses of bright neyron rose.

Regis. A compact miniature from the Monica Bennett strain. Dark foliage, profuse flowering with single salmon red flowers.

Susanne Screen. Large full trusses that do not shatter. White foundation with top two petals veined and suffused strongly with pink. All petals deeply margined and suffused rose. Single and well formed.

Nelly Waite. Another result of crossing into the American varieties. Pink with slight white eye and strong grower.

Mary Screen. A beautiful profuse single. Flowers have white foundation flushed with Dutch vermilion, petals inclined to frill. Winter flowering.

Elizabeth Bridge. A superb single magenta that beds and pots well.

Helen Bowie. A dwarf capable of producing a wealth of flowers of light mallow purple. Light green leaves with good zone. Single and winter flowering.

Kelvedon Beauty. Fine dwarf from Monica Bennett strain with more vigorous habit. Same dark foliage with profusion of lilac rose flowers. Awarded Silver Certificate, London 1971.

Marion Mason.   Striking bi-colour. Centre of pips white shading to pink, veined red with suffusion of post office red round the edges.

Tanya Richardson.   Good red double. Makes a fine standard.

Brutus.   An impulse seller with pips two inches across. Flowers all the year round under glass. Rich capsicum red with faint orange flush.

Bruce.   An exquisite white with fluted petals.

Debbie.   Double cherry red with white on upper petals. Awarded Bronze Medal, London.

Barbara Bennett.   Free grower. Long stems with single flowers empire rose, daintily feathered. Ideal for flower arrangers.

Elizabeth Bennett.   Single vivid neyron rose with white eye. Profuse flowering.

Betty Toles.   Single vivid cherry red with orange cast. Good for winter flowering.

Monica Bennett.   Dwarf zonal. Dark foliage. Amazing profusion of lilac pink flowers. Awarded Silver Medal London 1963.

Pink Sensation.   Vigorous sport from Doris Moore. Bright pink with white eye.

Pam Screen.   Rich velvety red single. Irresistible.

Beltane.   Beautiful bi-colour. Suffusion of pink on white foundation. Perfection of form.

Plato.   A magenta with delightful overlay of orange. Outstanding for bedding.

Staple White.   Pure white yielding a generous show of bloom even in winter under glass. Strong, healthy and desirable.

Stafford.   A rich clear pink single with white eye. Pips two inches across.

INDEX

COUNSELLING PEOPLE AT WORK

COUNSELLING PEOPLE AT WORK

An Introduction for Managers

Robert de Board

Gower

Published by
Gower Publishing Company Limited
Aldershot, Hants., England

British Library Cataloguing in Publication Data

De Board, Robert
    Counselling people at work.
    1. Employee counselling
    2. Personnel management
    I. Title
    658.3'85   HF5549.5.C8

    ISBN 0-566-02376-8

Typeset by Inforum Ltd, Portsmouth
Printed and bound in Great Britain by
Biddles Ltd, Guildford and King's Lynn

'The degree to which I can create relationships which facilitate the growth of others as separate persons is a measure of the growth I have achieved myself. In some respects this is a disturbing thought, but it is also a promising or challenging one. It would indicate that if I am interested in creating helping relationships I have a fascinating lifetime job ahead of me, stretching and developing my potentialities in the direction of growth.'

Carl Rogers, *On Becoming a Person*

———

'Only connect'

E. M. Forster, *Howards End*

Contents

Preface

This book is written primarily for managers who would like to be able to give effective help to people at work, especially their subordinates. Work can provide intense feelings of satisfaction and achievement, but it can also cause a number of problems which make people feel sad and miserable; and, for some, it can create anxiety and stress.

Most people find ways of coping with their bad times and this usually involves talking to someone, often their marriage partner, a close friend or a sympathetic doctor or clergyman. But I believe that people who have problems at work should be able to find help at work, and especially from their manager.

It is very difficult to give a precise definition of a manager and what he does, and this difficulty reflects the

subtle changes which have taken place in his role over the
years. One of these changes involves the shift in the relationship between a manager and his subordinates.
Attitudes to authority have changed significantly in the
last twenty years and no doubt will continue to change.
However, the manager still has the responsibility to get
work done through his staff and he is still ultimately
accountable for their performance. One of the great problems facing all organisations today is how a manager can
exercise his legitimate and necessary authority in a style
which is congruent with these changing attitudes.

It is my belief that the ability to counsel and to establish
a counselling relationship is now a necessary addition to
the managerial role and creates a management style
which is appropriate to the spirit of the age. The present-
day concept of counselling is a recent development and, in
fact, is ahead of the dictionaries, which usually define
counselling in terms of giving advice. According to the
British Association of Counselling, 'the task of counselling is to give the client an opportunity to explore, discover
and clarify ways of living more resourcefully and toward
greater well-being'.

How far managers can add counselling to their role
remains to be seen. In many company appraisal schemes,
the interview is called an 'appraisal and counselling'
interview but few managers receive any relevant guidance. Of course some managers do give effective and
appropriate help to their staff and no doubt there are
many people who counsel their boss! But, in my experience, these are exceptions rather than the rule.

In this book I have tried to explain what counselling
means in practice and I have given some theories and
ideas which help explain the process. I have tried to show
the advantages of counselling and some of the pitfalls. My
chief credential for writing this book is experience. Over
the last ten years I have spent part of my non-working life
as a counsellor and I currently spend time working with a
medical practice with referred clients. As a member of the
academic staff at Henley, The Management College, I am
involved in training managers in counselling skills and

these occasions are frequently the high spots on the programme. Not, I must add, because of what I do, but because
the managers find counselling interesting and
stimulating and often exciting. It can also be puzzling and
frustrating, but it is never dull, and the process of learning
about it is never finished.

A note about terminology

When a manager agrees to his subordinate's request for
help, an unwritten contract is formed. It therefore seems
appropriate, in the context of the counselling relationship
discussed in this book, to refer to the manager as 'counsellor' and to the subordinate as 'client'. These descriptions
do not, of course, imply that any financial transaction is
involved.

A manager may be approached by a variety of people for
help at work and he will respond in the ways he thinks
best. But this book will explore those situations where a
manager is asked for help by his subordinate who, in that
relationship, becomes his client.

Robert de Board

1

Styles of Helping

How do you react when someone asks you for help? As a
manager you may receive requests for help in a variety of
ways. Someone may pop their head round the door and say
'Can you spare me a minute?' or 'Are you busy?' A subordinate may ask to make a formal appointment and you
will book him or her in your diary for some time later that
day. Sometimes requests for help come about in less obvious ways. You may be talking to someone and their agitated or sad appearance may appear to be an unspoken
appeal for help, to which you could respond by saying 'You
look upset. Can I help?' Or it may be that in an appraisal
interview some aspect of your subordinate's performance
is concerning you and you ask him if there is a problem
about which he would like to talk to you.

Of course, every manager has the option *NOT* to give

help. You may be so busy that you don't want to be inter-
rupted. You may feel a lack of sympathy with the person
asking for help and feel that it is his job to solve his own
problems without getting you involved. Or you may be
perfectly aware that your subordinate is agitated and
upset, but you don't want to get involved in his personal
problems and so you give him no encouragement or opportunity to speak about them.

But let us suppose that you want to respond positively to
a request for help. What are your options? There are two
important factors which will affect the kind of help you
give.

1. Your concern for the client or your concern for the problem

Suppose you are a technical expert and a subordinate
comes to you with a tricky problem about which you have
expert knowledge. You will be very interested and concerned with the problem and you will want to get all the
facts in order to solve it. Your client (the subordinate) then
becomes of less importance to you than the problem. If, for
instance, I take my TV set to be repaired, I shall want the
electrician to concentrate on the fault and not be very
interested in me. In fact, I shall feel it inappropriate if he
starts asking me how I am feeling and tries to establish an
intimate relationship. In these instances, the helper is
problem-centred rather than client-centred.

On the other hand, if I am not feeling well and visit my
doctor for his help, I shall expect him to be concerned
about me as a person and not just interested in my symptoms. If he is a good doctor, he will be more client-centred
than problem-centred. But, if he is only concerned with
my symptoms and, like a technical expert, simply gives
me the pills and sends me packing, I shall not feel I have
got the kind of help I was looking for.

A manager who is asked for help can thus be problem-
centred or client-centred, and, as we shall see, these two
approaches result in different kinds of help being given.

2. Including or excluding the client in solving the problem

Once a problem has been presented to the manager for help he has the option to collaborate and involve the client or to exclude the client and work at the problem on his own. If, for instance, you have a tax problem and seek help from an accountant, he will ask for all the facts and then probably say 'Right, leave it with me and I'll write to you in a week'. You may be very happy with this approach and feel that it is money well spent to have the problem solved for you. A manager may take exactly the same approach to a subordinate's problem and even when the subordinate remains in the room, the manager can act entirely on his own and simply give the subordinate an answer, based on his own experience, attitudes and knowledge. On the other hand, the manager can collaborate and work with his subordinate so that the subordinate is included in the problem-solving process and has to use his own brains as they work together.

A manager who is asked for help can elect to take the problem over and solve it himself or he can decide to include the client in the problem-solving process. Each approach will result in a different kind of help being given.

To re-state the situation so far: when a manager is asked for help, he can respond in a variety of ways. His responses will depend mainly on two factors:

1. Where he will show his greatest concern. He can
   (a) be more concerned with the client, or
   (b) be more concerned with the problem.
2. How he will work with the client. He can
   (a) include the client in solving the problem, or
   (b) exclude the client from solving the problem.

When these factors are put together, it shows that the manager can adopt one of four basic styles of helping.

THE BASIC STYLES OF HELPING

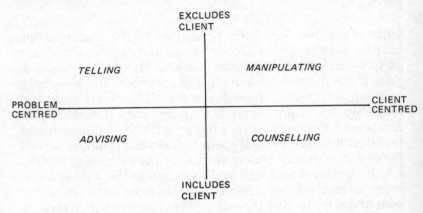

The four basic styles of helping are:

1. Telling   3. Manipulating
2. Advising   4. Counselling

Let us now look at each of them in more detail.

1. Telling

When the helper adopts the telling style he is more concerned with the problem than with the client and excludes the client from the problem-solving process. As we have already seen, this is the style most usually adopted by technical experts who are asked for help with technical problems. The helper takes over the problem and, having got as much information as possible, uses his expertise to solve it. Once he has got all the facts, he can virtually ignore his client, whom he then sees as a person awaiting an answer. People who typically adopt this style are lawyers, tax consultants, medical consultants and virtually any technical specialist, who all end up by telling their clients what to do. This is sometimes called the 'medical' model on the analogy of what happens when you go to a doctor for help, for example, with a broken arm. The doctor takes the problem over and you as a patient are only passively involved in the healing process. The arm is set and put in plaster and your problem returned to you solved. As the client you have learnt very little about the way the problem was solved and if you were ever to break an arm again, you would have to go through the same process and seek exactly the same kind of help.

People who adopt the telling approach to helping must have expert knowledge (or believe they have) and must be able fully to understand the problem presented to them. They must be able to come up with the correct solution and be prepared to take responsibility for the outcome. They must believe that they know what is best for the client. They will limit the client's involvement to the minimum, usually requiring him or her merely to provide information. On the whole, the helper who tells his client what to do wants to maintain him in a dependent position. He hopes that if problems occur in the future he will be asked for help again. The teller is not concerned with the client's learning or development and in some cases will deliberately keep the client in ignorance of the methods he uses. The teller is likely to use such words as: 'What you must do is . . .' or 'Follow these instructions.' or 'Don't argue. Do it this way.' or 'If things start to go wrong, call me immediately.' or 'When you have another problem, I want you to send for me.'

2. Advising

When the helper adopts the advising style, he is more concerned with the problem than the client, but wants to include him in the problem-solving process. The adviser will want to get all the facts and details about the problem and then, using his skills and experience, will usually come up with a number of options and alternatives. He will present these to the client, explain their strengths and weaknesses and then get his client to select the one he thinks most appropriate. This approach is typically used by business consultants who want their clients to be involved in the problem-solving process so that they will be committed to the solution and responsible for its implementation. This style of helping is sometimes called the 'teaching' model, for the client will learn something from this approach and it is the way in which many teachers work with their pupils, helping them to recognise and select the right answer from a limited number of options.

People who adopt the advising style of helping, whilst they want their client to be involved, still want to retain the role of specialist. They need their specialist knowledge and skills to help them come up with possible solutions and they are usually capable and willing to be involved in implementing the solution, once this is chosen and agreed with the client. However, the adviser is always pulled in two ways as he tries to give honest and objective help. The first pressure on him is to give solutions which he personally is capable of implementing. Business consultants and specialists within an organisation are likely to suggest solutions which will suit their own particular strengths and interests. For instance, a computer specialist is likely to suggest answers to a business problem which will involve computer systems, even though there may be a much simpler solution. Similarly, if you visit a doctor with a stomach upset he is likely to diagnose the problem in physical terms and offer help accordingly. However, a psychiatrist might see the same problem in terms of stress and anxiety and psychological symptoms and suggest a different kind of help.

The other pressure on the adviser is to make proposals which are likely to please his client and not offend him. For example, a business consultant involved in helping a manager to reorganise his business might suggest restructuring the company in a way which is beneficial to the client himself, giving him a higher position or a bigger empire; in fact, the client may well be part of the original business problem, but the consultant may think it politic not to say so.

The helper who adopts the advising style is likely to use such phrases as: 'It seems to me there are several things you could do.' or 'Why don't you . . .' or 'Which of my ideas appeal to you?' or 'These are the options open to you.' or 'My advice to you is . . .' or 'I'm sure you've chosen the right answer.' or 'I was hoping you'd say that. It's what I thought all along.'

3. Manipulating

When a helper adopts a manipulating style, he is apparently more concerned with the client than the problem but he excludes the client from the problem-solving process. This is essentially an unfair use of influence and usually means that the helper thinks he knows what is best for the client. This approach is often used by members of the worst sort of religious sect who believe that if only people would join them and adopt their beliefs, all their problems would be solved. In such cases, it is often the person who is apparently the helper who needs help the most. Under the guise of helping, he manipulates his client in order to satisfy his own needs and desires. People who use this style often have the erroneous belief that they are born 'helpers' and therefore seek out people whom they believe are in some kind of trouble. The manipulator needs to keep his client in this dependent role and by a variety of subtle means, makes his client think that he really needs him. Both helper and client play a game which can only have one result – the client becomes more and more dependent on his 'helper' and vice-versa, whilst the real problem remains unsolved.

Of course, all helpers need clients to carry out their legitimate work. A doctor needs his patients and a business consultant needs his executive clients. But the helper should always be working toward the time when he won't be needed. The proof of effective help is when the client can stand on his own two feet.

The manipulator often has a low opinion of his client and wants to change him, either to the image of himself, or to the kind of person he would like to have been. Manipulative helpers can be very dangerous and should be avoided like the plague. They can often be recognised by

the fact that they offer help before anyone has asked for it.
They are essentially salesmen who have a product to sell
and are continually looking for potential customers to buy
their wares. However, real help rarely comes in packages
and 'off-the-shelf' advice has little value. Such people are
likely to say 'Won't you let me help you?' or 'I've noticed
you're in trouble. I know just the thing for you.' or 'Why
don't we have a little talk?' or 'If I were you . . .'

4. Counselling

The helper who adopts a counselling style is more concerned with the client than with the problem and involves
the client in solving the problem. There are very significant differences between this style and the other three.

The first is that the counsellor need not have detailed
specialist knowledge about the problem presented to him
for help. Common sense suggests that he should have
enough awareness and knowledge to be able to ask intelligent and appropriate questions. But in the last analysis
his success in providing help depends more on his knowledge of human nature and his empathy with his client,
than on a detailed knowledge of the problem being discussed.

Secondly, he does not need to formulate a solution.
When he begins to counsel somebody he may have no idea
of the outcome and, indeed, may feel rather helpless himself.

The third important difference is that the aim of the
counsellor is to enable his client to find his own solution to
his problem. The helper who counsels does not take over
the problem in any way from his client. In fact, he helps
him to take full responsibility for it and is happy to withdraw as soon as possible. The counsellor never offers
advice and never criticises his client. He believes that the
client knows what is best for himself and helps him to
discover what this is. The counsellor listens rather than
talks, and uses his questioning skills to help his client
explore and analyse the problem in all its aspects.

Another difference between counselling and other forms of helping is that the counsellor wants the client to learn as much as possible through the problem-solving process, so that when he has another problem, he is much better equipped to deal with it himself. Because he is client-centred rather than problem-centred, he values his client as a person and is genuinely interested in his feelings and emotions and recognises that these are just as much connected with the problem as the more objective facts.

The counsellor is likely to use such phrases as: 'What seems to be the problem?' or 'Why is it worrying you?' or 'What do you think?' or 'How did that make you feel?' or 'Do you want to talk about it?' or 'If you do that, what do you think will happen?'

WHY USE COUNSELLING?

After reading this, many managers will recognise themselves as tellers and advisers. These are legitimate and effective ways of helping subordinates, and others, although it is clear that an effective helping style depends very much on the nature of the problem. Telling is a good response to a direct request for technical help. It is quick and results in the problem being solved and progress being made. In response to a request for advice, it may be appropriate to act as adviser and put forward good and viable solutions which the client may never have thought of himself, and allow him to select a course of action which now seems right to him. But what are the advantages of counselling? These are set out below.

1. Counselling is an effective way to help someone with their personal problems. Technical problems at work rarely worry people for long. There is usually an expert or a specialist on hand who – given the time and resources –

can come up with the right answer and tell or advise them
what to do.

But personal problems are different and require a different kind of help. For instance, a man approaching the
age of 50 who realises that he will not get further promotion may find the thought of another ten years in the
same job very depressing. As well as this, he may compare
his career progress with that of his contemporaries and
feel that he has done badly. This is a real problem which
will affect his performance and he may approach his boss
for help. What helping style should the boss adopt? Telling? 'Look here, Brian, you've got to get a grip on yourself,
and stop having these morbid thoughts. Get stuck into the
job and before you know it, it will be retirement time.' Or
advising? 'Brian, it seems to me you've got three options.
You could take early retirement at 55, which is only
another five years. Or you could hand in your notice now,
although I suppose you've still got the mortgage to pay.
Or, of course, you can always soldier on and hope things
improve. What do you think?'

A manager could take either of these approaches but it
is unlikey that they would provide any lasting help for the
depressed Brian. What he is looking for is someone who,
for a start, will listen to him and let him spill out his fears
and sadness, even though some if it may sound silly, even
to himself. He wants someone to show a real interest in
him so that he has the courage and strength really to
examine his situation and recognise all the implications.
And then he wants help to explore the opportunities open
to him so that he can make up his own mind about what he
should do.

In other words, he is looking for a counsellor. The problem is whether he can find one or not. He may be able to
get this kind of help from a clergyman or an understanding GP. Perhaps he has a wife who can give him wise
counsel. But the concern of this book is that he should get
this kind of help from his boss.

The above example is only one of the hundreds of personal problems which affect people at work. Each unresol-

ved problem of this kind not only adds to the sum of human unhappiness, but also reduces people's efficiency.

Counselling is a way of helping people deal with their personal problems in a way which telling or advising can never achieve.

2. Counselling results in decisions that 'stick'. When people are offered help, there are essentially four ways in which they can react.

(a) They can reject help.

(b) They can accept the help and advice because they are coerced into accepting it. If they don't accept, they fear they may incur the displeasure of the helper who may operate some sort of sanction against them. Some managers who are tellers and advisers can get very upset and even angry if their solutions are not accepted, even when they are offering help with sensitive personal matters. So their subordinates accept their proposals because they feel forced to do so.

(c) They accept the help offered because they like and respect the helper and in some way identify with him. Some helpers are very charismatic and seem to exude an air of mystical wisdom. However, there are very few charismatic managers, and trying to be liked by everyone is an exhausting business. And when it happens, as it must, that the charismatic helper is discovered to have feet of clay, he loses all credibility.

(d) They accept the help offered because they themselves have been enabled to work through the problem and are pesonally involved in the final decision and solution. They have gone through the process of internalising, that is, taking the ideas inside themselves and making them their own. When this happens, the individual is committed to implementing the solution, not because anyone has forced him to do so, but because he has made a personal decision. This process of internalising results from counselling: the client says 'I did it myself', and he is determined to carry out the solution he himself has reached.

3. Counselling results in human growth and development. People who, when they seek help, are always told or advised what to do, can never grow. All they learn is whom to ask for help. But counselling, because it forces the client to think for himself, can provide him with opportunities for growth and, more importantly, with opportunities for change. Some adults have difficulty abandoning the patterns of behaviour established in childhood: they may look for helpers who will behave like parents and treat them like children, giving them either love and praise or criticism and punishment.

Counselling can break this pattern and enable people to think for themselves and make decisions that are right for them. Counselling helps them to face the reality of their own autonomy and enables them to realise that they are free to choose. The counsellor is not a father-figure, but simply an adult working with another adult who has neither to be pleased nor feared. Managers who can achieve this kind of relationship with their subordinates and provide help through counselling, enable them to grow and develop in ways which no training course can ever achieve.

4. Counselling is in tune with changing attitudes towards authority. There is no doubt that society in Britain and in many other countries has undergone profound changes in the last 30 years. The old authority figures, such as clergymen, doctors and the aristocracy, no longer demand or obtain automatic respect. Political leaders are more likely to be criticised than praised. There is a much greater demand for participation and involvement in decision-making at all levels of society. People increasingly challenge authority: 'Why should I? Who does he think he is?' These attitudes are encouraged by the educational system which says 'Think for yourself. Make up your own mind.'

However, in spite of the increasing challenge to authority, people still need leaders and leadership as much as they ever did. In spite of widespread cynicism and disillusion with politics, the selection and appointment of leaders, such as a prime mininster or president, send a country into a paroxysm of anxiety, while the death of a Pope and the selection of his successor are of immense international concern. At the parochial level, the appointment of leaders in any kind of organisation, from the gardening club to the village preservation society, still creates intense activity and can turn gentle citizens into furious campaigners.

When one leader goes and a new one has yet to be appointed, people really do feel leaderless; whether it concerns their church or their country it worries and frightens them. Groups and societies need leaders if only to criticise and attack, and the lack of one arouses the emotions and creates intense anxiety. One of the problems facing leaders today is how to find a leadership style that is appropriate to these changing social attitudes and yet allows them to exercise their legitimate authority.

The manager faces exactly the same dilemma. His work team is likely to have these anti-authoritarian attitudes and will expect to be increasingly consulted and involved with what is going on. They want to challenge established systems and procedures and to examine any new proposals and changes. They do not want passively to accept orders and are unlikely to give automatic respect to their manager.

And yet they want leadership. They need a manager who is visibly seen to be in charge and who they know carries the ultimate responsibility for their group. They want a manager who has evolved a leadership style which recognises and adapts to their attitudes and who, at the same time, is effective and gets the job done.

The image of the old-style 'hire-and-fire' boss, the bullying autocrat, is as abhorrent to most managers as it is to the workforce. The struggle for many managers today is how to find a style which takes into account current attitudes and yet enables them to exercise their proper and necessary authority.

Counselling is one way of doing this. It allows the manager to show a real concern for the people working for him. It enables him to facilitate their growth and development. It allows him to recognise and communicate the bounds of

his authority and to make his subordinates realise the
real and inevitable consequences of crossing them. It provides his subordinates with opportunities to analyse and
clarify problems and create and test new ideas and ways or
working.

SUMMARY

When a manager is asked for help by a subordinate his response will depend on two factors.
(a) His concern for the subordinate himself or the problem he brings. Will he be client-centred or problem-centred?
(b) The way in which he works on the problem, either on his own or with the client. Will he include or exclude him in the problem-solving process?
When these factors are combined it can be seen that there are four basic helping styles which anyone can adopt and each will have a different effect: telling, advising, manipulating and counselling.

1. Telling

The person who gives help by telling his client what to do, is problem-centred and excludes the client from the problem-solving process. This style is frequently adopted by technical experts whose skill and knowledge enable them to give the right answer.

2. Advising

The person who helps by giving advice is problem-centred and includes his client in problem-solving. The adviser frequently develops options and then gets the client to select the one he favours. The danger is that he will offer solutions which require his own expertise and which will not offend his client.

3. Manipulating

The person who uses a manipulating style is apparently client-centred but in fact excludes the client from the problem-solving process. Such a person uses his client to satisfy his own needs and wants to keep him in a highly-dependent role. Manipulative helpers can often be recognised by the fact that they offer help before anyone has requested it.

4. Counselling

Counselling is a style of helping which is client-centred and involves the client in solving the problem. It is significantly different from the other three styles and aims to help the client find solutions to his own problems.

WHY USE COUNSELLING?

Telling and advising people how to solve their problems can be effective ways for managers to give help, especially when the problems are technical ones. But counselling has specific advantages over the other helping styles.

1. It provides effective help with personal problems. When a subordinate has a personal problem he is looking for someone who can help him explore what is troubling him and eventually help him make up his own mind what he should do. Unresolved problems not only cause unhappiness but also reduce efficiency, and counselling is an effective way to deal with this.
2. It results in decisions that 'stick'. A person at work will only be committed to making a change in his attitude or behaviour if he has personally thought the problem through and reached his own decision. Good counselling enables this process of internalisation to take place, resulting in the subordinate being determined to carry out the changes he himself has decided upon.
3. It results in growth and development. Counselling helps and encourages people to think for themselves.

Through being involved in the problem-solving process, the client learns more about himself, develops his own resources and abilities, and becomes better equipped to manage future problems.

4. It is in tune with current social attitudes. In an age when authority is questioned and where the education system encourages a 'make-up-your-own-mind' attitude, there is still a real need for leadership. Counselling is one way in which a manager can exercise his authority effectively but in a non-authoritarian manner.

2

Predicting People's Problems

All managers have to solve problems. Their professional training and experience are geared to improving their problem-solving ability. When promotion comes it always involves an increased responsibility for solving bigger and better problems. A problem in managerial terms is any situation where reality differs from expectations in an adverse way. For instance, there is a problem in cash flow when revenue is less than the planned amount. There is a production problem when output is less than predicted and there is a problem with supplies when what is available is less than required.

It might be expected that as managerial skills in problem-solving increase and are added to the total experience of organisations, fewer problems would occur, or that those which do occur would be solved more easily.

It might seem, in other words, that as the body of managerial knowledge grows, the reality of business life should become closer to management's plans and forecasts. Paradoxically, this does not appear to be the case. Many managers would argue that, in fact, their problems are increasing in number and complexity. The micro-chip may well herald a new industrial revolution but it will also bring many managerial headaches. The electronic office will need an old-fashioned medicine cabinet for the aspirin. Fritz Schumacher, author of *Small is Beautiful*, pointed out this same paradox with regard to science in his last book, *Good Work,* (p.98):

> Another illusion which is still rampant is that science can solve all problems. I have no doubt that science can solve any individual problem when it is clearly defined. But my experience is that as it solves problem 'A', it creates a whole host of new problems. It's quite a thought that there are more scientists alive today than there have been in all previous human history taken together. What do they all do? They solve problems very efficiently. Aren't we running out of problems? No. We have more and more. This seems to be a bottomless pit. They grow faster than we solve them. So this is where we have to ask 'What on earth is going on here?'

So, what on earth is going on in organisations, when there are more and more managers who have never been so well educated and trained and yet the problems facing them are increasing both in number and complexity?

One way to answer this question is to look at the kinds of problems facing managers and these, I suggest, fall into two main categories, (a) technical and, (b) human. These are the twin aspects of every manager's job and yet it is remarkable that the human one still comes a very poor second in the real world of business. Although there is an explosion of books on psychology and courses about behavioural science, the technical aspect of work is still seen to be the main managerial task in most factories and offices. Promotions to executive posts are usually made on the criterion of technical ability. A senior director was once heard to say 'I don't give a damn if he's good with people or not. Can he get those car bodies moving off the production line?'

This idea is particularly prevalent in the professions. Scientists, engineers and accountants, for instance, undertake long and exhaustive technical training, and consequently tend to judge people's performance solely in terms of technical skill. Yet it is common experience that as a person moves up through an organisation, he is involved less and less in technical work and more with the human problems of leadership, co-operation and the co-ordination of other people's work.

Can 'people-problems' be predicted in organisations or must managers continue to be surprised and perplexed by the problems that seem continually to face them? Undoubtedly the basic predictors are those learnt through experience: an intelligent manager learns to recognise the pattern of events and situations which usually result in problems and so takes avoiding action. But experience takes time to acquire and is, by definition, not available to the young or newly appointed manager; furthermore, not everyone has the inclination or ability to learn from their experience.

As well as experience, however, there are a number of ideas and theories which are helpful in trying to predict when and where people-problems may occur. Elliott Jacques has proposed the idea that people at work will be problem free (he calls this a state of 'psychological equilibrium') when the work they do is just matched by their capacity to do it and for that work they receive payment which is felt to be equitable. Thus, there are clearly three areas which can cause problems:

(a) When people feel their pay is unequitable for the work they do and the responsibilities they carry. It should be noted that this includes feeling overpaid as well as the more obvious feeling of underpayment.

(b) The nature and content of the work itself. Is it too easy or too demanding?

(c) The capacity of the individual to carry out the work he is given to do.

Using these three concepts, Jacques is able to describe 12 possible situations which can cause a person at work to feel dissatisfaction and therefore to have a personal problem ('Equitable Payment' Chapter 12).

Another fruitful source of ideas which can help managers predict people-problems is in the writing of Freud. In *Group Psychology and the Analysis of the Ego* (Chapter 1) he attempts to analyse the processes which occur when a group or an organisation form. He says that there are two important factors in this process:

(a) Leadership – the group coalesces around a leader and therefore the group cannot form until his authority is established and accepted.

(b) Interpersonal relations – once everyone accepts the leader, they then have a common focus and can form relationships with each other.

I have personally found this idea to have the greatest practical value when working with groups or consulting with organisations. I believe I can now predict that when there are serious problems preventing a group from working, it will involve either the authority of the leader ('Who does he think he is?' 'How did he get appointed?'), or bad relations between the members ('How do they think I could work with so and so?' 'I can't stand his attitude').

There are, of course, many other theories and ideas which can help in prediction, especially those concerning motivation and satisfaction. For instance, Herzberg's famous 'Motivation – Hygiene' theory can provide a checklist of factors which may cause a person to have a problem, such as poor supervision, bad working conditions, lack of responsibility, and so on.

CATEGORISING PEOPLE-PROBLEMS

If a person at work has a problem, what is likely to be causing it? Excluding those problems which can be solved by the application of technical skills, i.e. plant breakdown,

computer malfunction, etc., people-problems can be
grouped into (at least) three categories:
- Personality problems
- Organisational problems
- External problems.

1. Personality problems

Some people have problems or can cause them, simply by
the way they are and the way they behave. They may be
worried and depressed by lack of confidence or feelings of
unworthiness, or else they may be arrogant and
dominating, continually causing rows and upsets. The
problems caused by these kinds of behaviour arise not
from the organisation, but from the individual. He carries
this way of behaving around with him, no matter where he
works or what he does. In many ways, these problems are
the most difficult to solve and cause the greatest difficulties at work. Table 1 outlines types of behaviour which
may indicate that the problem is of this nature.

2. Organisational problems

Many people-problems are the direct result of human
beings living and working together in the same organisation. Anyone can tell if they have an organisational problem by simply asking the question 'Would I still have this
problem if I left this organisation?' If the answer is 'no',
then it is an organisational problem.

Problems of this kind can be fairly well predicted on the
basis of past experience, together with some of the
theories and ideas mentioned previously. They are likely
to be caused by issues of authority, poor interpersonal
relations, payment not felt to be equitable, overwork,
boredom, lack of promotion and so on.

Because these problems are a function of the organisation, they should all be capable of being resolved within it.
Regretfully this is rarely so. Many organisations have

grown so quickly and have been so engrossed with their progress, or else have been so badly managed, that they have failed to develop this self-correcting mechanism. All too often an organisation is judged to be healthy and dynamic on such crude criteria as profits or technological advancement. I believe that for success in the future, all organisations will have to devise ways in which organisational people-problems can be solved – or at least helped – within the organisation. Those that don't will suffer the same fate as the dinosaurs, doomed to extinction because they failed to adapt to the changing environment.

There is some hard evidence concerning the problems which people have at work. In the early 1920s the Western Electric Company in Chicago initiated a unique programme of research into the effect of work on human performance. This was supervised by Professor Elton Mayo and his colleagues from Harvard and is known generally as the 'Hawthorne Experiments' (Dickson and Roethlisberger, 1966).

One part of this work was a long-term programme of counselling which lasted from 1936 to 1955. The counsellors were full-time independent professionals and were not part of management. The programme started with five counsellors and this number steadily increased until 1948 when there were 55 counsellors covering a workforce of 21,000. From then on, the number of counsellors began to fall and when the programme ended in 1955 there were only eight.

The terms of reference were very wide. Any employee could request an interview with his counsellor, and the counsellor could request an interview with an employee. Confidentiality was maintained and complete records were kept of all the interviews. For what reasons did employees visit the counsellors? When the reports were analysed, they revealed that the counselling sessions dealt mainly with the following five concerns of employees:

1 Keeping and losing a job
2 Unsatisfactory work relations

Problem	Minor	Serious	Acute/Chronic
POOR SELF—IMAGE AND A HIGH OPINION OF OTHERS	Humble, timid, anxious to please, unsure of himself, uncertain of the future. Wants to 'help' rather than to 'do'. Tells anecdotes of his past mistakes and blunders. Easily influenced. Always searching for a 'real' friend.	Cannot accept success or achievement. Worries over possible failure. Seeks excuses for avoiding responsibility. Indecisive. Dependent. Wants a 'special' relationship rather than group membership.	Opts out of decision - making Withdraws from personal relationships. Cynical about making improvements. Envious of others' achievements. Suffers from depression.
OVER—ESTIMATION OF OWN ABILITY	Talks at you. Very definite views. Aggressive. Ready to take people on. Looks out for fools so as not to suffer them gladly. Dominates meetings. Has a temper. Boring.	Autocratic, not open to influence, fixed views on all issues. Critical of colleagues and subordinates. Boastful. Makes quick decisions. Dislikes participation. Won't delegate. Gets angry. Wants to control others.	Bullying, arrogant. Ignores facts, plays hunches. Contemptuous of other people. Enjoys triumphing over others. Won't tolerate criticism. High blood pressure.
POOR SELF—IMAGE AND LOW OPINION OF OTHERS	Self-pitying, anxious, muddled. Poor work organisation. Blames others for own mistakes. Worried that 'they' may be watching him. Few friends.	Confused and inconsistent. Increasing load of unfinished work. Forgetful. Fairly sure that 'they' are getting at him. Defensive, lonely. Secretive.	Irrational. Work organisation chaotic. Jobs never completed. Isolated. Paranoid. Heading for 'breakdown'

Table 1. Personality problems – behaviour predictors

3   Felt injustices
4   Unsatisfactory relations with authority
5   Job development.

(You will recall that Freud's theory of group behaviour showed that interpersonal relationships and authority issues were likely to be significant major factors. Items 2 and 4 give empirical evidence for this.)

However, it is my experience that the principal causes of anxiety within organisations can be classified as follows:

— Technical incompetence
— Underwork (role underload)
— Overwork (role overload)
— Uncertain future
— Relationships.

Every individual will reveal his anxiety in his own way, but it is to some extent possible to generalise, and Table 2 sets out some of the behaviour characteristics one might expect to observe in people with problems of this kind.

3. External problems

For every employee in an organisation, at whatever level, work is only one part of life. The three major parts of life are work, family and leisure: but they are each part of the same life lived by the same person. Each of these parts of life have a profound effect on the total person and his behaviour, wherever he is and whatever he is doing. When a person is at work, he inevitably brings with him the emotions and feelings generated from outside and of course when he leaves the office or factory, he takes with him the effect of these work experiences. This continual interplay and interchange goes some way to explaining the varied and sometimes extraordinary problems which people will confide to their manager.

How far a manager should go in dealing with problems of a personal or even intimate nature will depend on the individual manager and the relationship he has with the

	Minor	Serious	Acute/Chronic
TECHNICAL INCOMPETENCE	Unsure of some work or office procedures or technical processes and systems.	Unable to grasp all details of processes and systems for which he is accountable. Has made, or at least fears he will make, a serious error.	Cannot assimilate new ideas and technology. Unable, or unwilling to make decisions. Bad relations with technical experts and new graduates. Frequently absent with bilious attacks.
UNDERWORK	Occasionally bored by lack of work or work that is undemanding.	Feels continually bored and talents underemployed. Concerned by lack of demanding work. Always reads 'job vacancies' in the paper. Begins to have poor timekeeping record.	Casual or cynical attitude to work. Nothing seems important Increased pre-lunch drinking. Weekend starts on Thursday. Projects never get completed. Increased flirtation.
OVERWORK	Sometimes over-whelmed by pressure of work, sudden panics and crises.	Continually attending meetings, always on the phone, takes work home. Too much travelling. Everything is urgent and needed yesterday. Social life contracting. Always tired.	Continually agitated. Loss of contact with staff. Works longer hours but backlog of work increasing. Sleeps badly and has increasing rows at home. Social life vanishing. Starts to take Valium.
UNCERTAIN FUTURE	Concerned about next promotion move. When and where to?	Worried by lack of promotion. Younger people moving past him. Has he reached his ceiling? Soothing noises from boss, but no definite statement of career plans.	Frightened by lack of promotion. Undertakes more and more work to prove his ability. Envious of colleagues' status and possessions. Increasing bank overdraft to 'keep up with the Jones's'
RELATIONSHIPS	Concerned by lack of friends at work and the feeling of not belonging.	Feels isolated and ignored. Attempts at friendship seem to fail. Has a poor self-image and worries about lack of qualifications. Increased paranoia. Are they 'getting at him?'	Increasingly withdrawn. Eats lunch on his own. Sarcastic and cynical about the organisation. His department appears increasingly chaotic. At meetings negative and uncooperative. Avoids personal contacts—uses memos.

Table 2.   Organisational problems – behaviour predictors

subordinate. Every manager learns to recognise the problems he can cope with and those which he should refer to another, possibly more professional, agency. However, the effective counsellor learns never to be surprised at the oddness of human behaviour or the intricate and seemingly stupid situations into which people can get themselves.

Marriage By far the largest number of problems arising outside work are related to marriage. Every counsellor needs to recognise that couples live 'happily ever after' only in stories, and that any marriage is likely to have as many bad times as good. He will also know that there are always two sides to these problems and that he is only hearing one of them. He realises that by 'taking sides' he would be compounding the problem; his job is rather to help the person explore and understand the total situation. This friendly but essentially neutral approach is difficult to maintain, especially if the manager knows the family concerned and is friendly with them. But from my own experience, this is the most helpful approach. The worst approach of all is for the manager, albeit with the best of motives, to agree with all the person says, thus colluding with him. This may well contribute to a deterioration in the situation.

Bereavement The death of a close friend or relative, and especially the death of a partner, is one of the hardest blows anyone can suffer. Death has replaced sex as society's 'tabu' subject and many people are embarrassed when they meet someone who has recently been bereaved. They usually give what appears to be good advice and encourage the person to keep working and to make sure they are always busy. But in fact what every bereaved person needs to do is to mourn the loss of their loved one. Less sophisticated societies than ours know the truth of this and have ceremonies and rituals which allow for and encourage an open show of grief. There is a lot of evidence to show that people who are unable to mourn, or are discouraged from doing so, store up all kinds of psychological problems for the future.

Bereavement can bring about a variety of feelings which may include sadness, anger and guilt; these all take time to be expressed and worked through. It is interesting to note that Freud speaks of the 'work of mourning' to indicate that it requires a great deal of mental and emotional energy and effort.

Helpful counselling for a bereaved person allows him or her to talk about the person who has died and possibly the circumstances surrounding the death. Often the anger felt at a death is not simply due to the loss of a loved one, but anger at a world that doesn't notice and doesn't care.

Of course, death is a frightening and fearful thing and any death causes us, in some way, to be aware of our own mortality. As John Donne wrote, 'Never send to know for whom the bell tolls. It tolls for thee.' A counsellor who can offer a person the opportunity to talk about his bereavement, within a supportive and caring relationship, is providing the most valuable help.

This sort of counselling requires the ability to talk of death without getting upset oneself and also not to be anxious at the expression of grief. In one incident, a manager came rushing out of his office, looking very distraught, saying 'Come quick. Jack's broken down!' What had happened was that Jack was crying! An effective counsellor will not be frightened if the person breaks down and cries. Rather, he knows that this is good and that he is enabling that person to come to grips with his own sadness and gradually work through it.

Depression Depression is an 'umbrella' term used to cover a variety of painful emotional states. It may refer to a passing mood of 'being down in the dumps' or to a more or less permanent state of misery. There are clearly many situations which are sad and depressing and everyone experiences feelings of depression at some time. This is called 'reactive' depression and may result from a bereavement, the loss of a job, failure to get promotion, a marriage break-up, etc. Counselling someone who is suffering from this kind of depression requires great skill and sensitivity, and the manager may feel that he is not

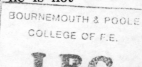

equipped to cope. However, it is hard to know who *is* equipped to cope! Not every doctor has the time or skill to listen, and the result is an enormous number of prescriptions for anti-depressant drugs – which can never solve the problem.

Counselling is difficult in these cases because when people are very depressed their whole view of themselves and of the world becomes negative and pessimistic. Everything is interpreted in terms of gloom and failure and even the most joyful events are experienced in terms of unhappiness. The counsellor must listen attentively and sympathetically, and, by asking sensitive questions, allow the person to explore his feelings. The more the person can be helped to explore the reality of his problem, the sooner will he start to come to terms with his feelings and begin to consider doing something about them. Under no circumstances will the counsellor tell the person to 'snap out of it': he realises that this is not possible.

There is a more serious form of depression called 'endogenous' depression, which is an illness, and appears not to be linked with any obvious event or cause. This form of illness affects probably one in fifteen of the population and clearly needs professional help.

> The typical depression seen in older, obsessive people is characterised by continual tiredness, lack of drive, finding everything an effort and feeling worse in the mornings and better as the day wears on. Sleep is disturbed by early morning waking, often with a sense of dread. Appetite, weight and sexual drive are reduced. There is a lack of initiative, a tendency to worry about trivia, a gloomy outlook which disturbs judgement and loss of normal aggressiveness. There is a tendency to drink more alcohol and to smoke more heavily.
>
> (*The BMA Book of Executive Health*)

The causes of this illness are still uncertain. It may be due to a chemical imbalance and it frequently does respond to chemotherapy. It may also be due to unconscious psychological processes with unexpressed feelings which result in feelings of self-hatred. If the manager thinks that a subordinate is suffering from severe depression, he should urge that person to seek professional advice, which, in the first instance, means consulting his G.P.

Fortunately these illnesses have an excellent prognosis with treatment and once the individual has recovered there is no impairment of psychological integrity. It is worth repeating here that such illnesses are not necessarily a result of work difficulty, although to the sick patient work becomes an intolerable burden and may be blamed. There are many other precipitants, from unexpressed grief or anger, the effect of certain drugs including alcohol and after-effects of severe infections or surgical operations, to the effect of hormones, including in some women the contraceptive pill. It is important to consider such possibilities carefully before reducing the level of responsibility of someone who may have spent much of his life attaining a position that, with help, he is still capable of fulfilling. *(The BMA Book of Executive Health)*

SUMMARY

A. Solving problems is an integral part of every manager's job and each promotion brings responsibility for solving bigger and more complex ones. In spite of improved management education, problems at work seem to increase rather than decrease. This is because the problems which cause managers the greatest worry and concern usually involve human factors. There are some useful theories and ideas which can help managers predict possible problem situations.

1. Elliott Jaques suggests that three factors must be in balance if a person is to be in a state of 'psychological equilibrium'. These are:
(a) An equitable payment (i.e. payment that is felt to be fair)
(b) The content of the work itself
(c) The capacity of the individual.
2. Freud argues that a group or organisation must resolve two important issues before it can work effectively. These are:
(a) The authority and position of the leader
(b) The interpersonal relationships between the members.
3. Herzberg's 'Motivation – Hygiene' theory indicates that dissatisfaction is likely to arise from the 'Hygiene Factors', which comprise company policy and administration, supervision, salary, interpersonal relations and working conditions.

B. People-problems fall into three categories: personality, organisational and external problems.

1. Personality problems stem from the nature of the individual himself and manifest themselves in the way he behaves, no matter where he is. These problems may arise because an individual has:
(a) A poor self-image but a high opinion of others
(b) An over-estimation of his own abilities

(c) A poor self-image and a low opinion of other people.

2. Organisational problems: these kinds of people-problems are the direct result of people living and working together in the same organisation. They should therefore be capable of being resolved within the organisation and counselling is one way of doing this.

In a 20-year counselling programme in the USA an analysis showed that employees visited their counsellors with five primary concerns:

(a) Keeping and losing a job
(b) Unsatisfactory work relations
(c) Felt injustices
(d) Unsatisfactory relations with authority
(e) Job development.

Another classification of organisational problems are:

(a) Technical incompetence
(b) Underwork (role underload)
(c) Overwork (role overload)
(d) Uncertain future
(e) Relationships.

3. External problems: problems that arise outside the organisation can obviously affect performance at work. How far a manager should be prepared to offer help on these personal and intimate problems depends on his relationship with the person in trouble and the confidence he has in his own counselling abilities. These problems can be many and various, but frequently include:

(a) Marriage
(b) Bereavement
(c) Depression.

REFERENCES

Dickson, J.D., and Roethisberger, F.J., *Counselling in an Organisation,* Harvard University, Boston, 1966
Jaques, E., *Equitable Payment,* Heinemann, 1961 (Especially Chapter 5 'Conditions for Psycho-Economic equilibrium')
Freud, S., *Group Psychology and the Analysis of the Ego,* Hogarth Press (Standard Edition of the complete works of Sigmund Freud), 1959
Schumacher, F., *Good Work,* Cape, 1979

3

The Elements of Counselling

The prime aim of counselling is to help the individual discover the solutions to his own problems. This may go against a natural inclination to give advice, especially in a boss-subordinate relationship. People only become committed to a particular decision or course of action when they have made up their own minds and personally believe that it is the right thing to do. This fact is at the centre of positive motivation. Whilst money, conditions, and the type of work are all contributory factors to the motivation of people at work, the essential factor is the personal commitment which a person brings to their work. When it becomes 'my work' and not 'his work', I start working for myself and use all my own internal energy and standards and enjoy all the potential psychological rewards. The effective counsellor acknowledges this process and attempts to work with it.

What is right for me is not necessarily right for someone else and what is important to me is not automatically important to others. The counsellor recognises an individual's autonomy and potential power, attempts to realise and release this power, rather than to deny or fight it. In a counselling interview between a manager and his subordinate, the manager recognises that his own power and authority are important factors. Equally important are the subordinate's own standards and aspirations and the potential energy they can release.

Counselling aims to help a person find his own solution to a problem. Set out below are some important aspects of effective counselling.

Listening

Listening need not be passive activity and Carl Rogers has coined the description 'active listening'. This means doing something positive rather than simply refraining from talking! It involves an attitude of mind and body which sends out the non-verbal message to the person being counselled: 'At this moment you are the most important person in my world. What you are saying interests and concerns me. You have my full attention.' Different people will do this in different ways but there will be certain things common to all. There will be plenty of eye contact. There will be no interruptions until the person has obviously finished speaking. The counsellor will be physically alert, indicating a genuine interest in what is being said.

Perhaps the biggest obstacle to active listening is the desire to think ahead and plan the next question. The counsellor communicates that this is happening by a variety of signals which together say 'I want to interrupt now'; he withdraws his attention from what the person is saying and gives it to the question he is forming.

Active listening has at least two positive benefits in counselling. The first and obvious one is that it provides information for further discussion and action. The second is that it undoubtedly has a therapeutic effect. Talking to an attentive listener enables people to externalise their problems, which is the first step to getting rid of them, and it can give great emotional release. Linked with this is the confirmation which an attentive listener automatically gives to a speaker, of their importance as a person.

The 'presenting' problem

It can be difficult to start a counselling interview. The way in which this happens depends on the relationship which already exists between the manager and his subordinate and also on the problems which both hope, or fear, will be discussed. However, from the subordinate's point of view, the more serious or delicate the issue he wishes to raise, the more difficulty he will find in broaching it. His first words are unlikely to be a full statement of the problem. He will find it easier to start by stating the problem in broad terms, in such a way that the boss is unlikely to react sharply. Consciously or unconsciously, he will be saying sufficient to enable him to go further, if the climate feels 'right', or if necessary, to withdraw without having given too much away. He may be struggling internally, seeing how much he can admit to himself and what defence mechanisms he can cease to operate.

The practical response required from the counsellor in this situation is to listen intently and be prepared to help the subordinate open up and go further towards the heart of the matter.

Finding the core problem

This follows naturally from understanding the difficulty of presenting the problem. Statements made by the subordinate at the start of a counselling interview, always contain clues, or linkages, to the essence of the problem — the thing which is concerning him personally at that very moment. Statements such as 'I'm worried about the paperwork at the office', or 'I'm concerned with the poor relationships in the department', are generalities which, if taken as the full statement of the problem would result in non-effective action. A good counsellor will understand the reason for the general statement and by appropriate questions, enable the person to speak of the core problem; this will always be something to do with his personal situation at the present time, and will usually involve some other person or persons.

Recognising and admitting feelings

Every problem brought for counselling is concerned with a person's feelings. Problems that are purely technical don't require counselling, but can be solved by factual answers. (However, it should be noted that a problem which is presented as a purely technical one may frequently have an emotional aspect as well.) The exploration and recognition of emotions can be extremely difficult for a manager. Part of a subordinate's problem may be the fear of not being up to the job, or the fear of redundancy. Or it could be that he feels anxious about his promotion prospects or salary level. Whatever the problem, an effective counsellor knows that it cannot be fully resolved unless or until the associated 'feelings' have been dealt with. The subordinate must be given not only the opportunity to express his feelings, which he may be in the habit of concealing, but also the help to explore and clarify what these are. This kind of counselling work requires sensitivity, but in my own experience it is the key to effectiveness, and results in problem resolution, personal growth and self-insight.

Criticism

The one thing guaranteed to stop effective counselling is criticism. When people are criticised, they feel threatened and the automatic psychological responses are fight or flight. The fight response is obvious enough and may take the form of 'What do you mean, my work's not up to scratch? You're never around to see it!' The flight response is usually a little more subtle but it involves moving on from the topic as quickly as possible. It might involve an apology – 'I'm very sorry, it won't happen again' – or else a string of excuses. Either way the person who feels criticised is putting into operation his defence mechanisms to protect himself from the perceived threat. The climate of openness and trust, essential for effective counselling, has changed and it takes a long time for it to be re-established. The interview may continue, but no further useful work will be done.

Some managers find this difficult to accept, believing that it may be appropriate to criticise a subordinate. Criticism may have its uses, but in the counselling relationship, it is simply counter-productive.

Problem-solving

Counselling is all about helping people to solve their own problems. But the situation is rarely clear cut – presumably if it were so, then there would be no problem. Whilst no formula can be given for a counselling interview, it is likely to contain the following elements (not necessarily in this order):

1. The presenting problem
2. Finding the core problem
3. Discovering why it is a problem
4. Exploration of feelings
5. Examining possible solutions and alternatives
6. Recognising their implications
7. Deciding on a course of action (including 'no-action').

The counsellor will only achieve an interview of this kind if he asks open-ended, pertinent questions. All the questioning words, like how, what, when, where, and why, enable the person to explore his own world, to clarify the

problem, to consider solutions and realise their implications.

Authoritarian people sometimes dismiss non-directive
counselling as a soft option, because they think it helps
people to avoid the truth, which may be harsh. But in fact,
the effective counsellor can ask questions which would
otherwise be avoided and, with sensitivity, can enter areas
which normally read 'keep out'.

Choosing the direction

Counselling is in some way an exploration, but it is necessary for the counsellor to steer the interview in the right
direction, that is, the direction that will lead to the resolution of the problem. But what is the 'right' direction?
There is no simple answer to this question, but it is a fact
that the counsellor takes the discussion into different
areas by his choice of question or response. He may move
down a path which turns out to be a dead end and the cost
may simply be the waste of a certain amount of time. On
the other hand, inappropriate questioning may result in
undue significance being attached to a problem of minor
importance, the resolution of which brings very little
benefit and leaves the real problem untouched.

The effective counsellor continually constructs mental
hypotheses and uses these as the basis for giving a direction to the discussion. The word 'hypothesis' – temporary
and tentative explanation which seems to fit the facts so
far, but which may be changed in the light of new and
different information – is important. The counsellor,
working in this way, is continually computing the facts
and feelings which he is hearing and perceiving, and tes-
ting them against the hypothesis he is forming. This leads
him to take a line of approach which enables the person
being counselled to explore and examine a particular
aspect of the situation and maybe gain new knowledge
and insight about himself in the process. The ensuing
conversation may then confirm the counsellor's
hypotheses and so enable him to go further down that

particular avenue. If however, the opposite happens, then he rejects that idea and searches for another that is more probable.

This skill of asking the right questions is directly related to the counsellor's knowledge of human behaviour and especially his awareness of the range of human feelings and emotions. If he has an understanding of all the kinds of factors which are likely to be contributing to the problem, then he can construct wide-ranging hypotheses which are more likely to be helpful and lead to the core of the problem. If, on the other hand his general understanding of human behaviour is narrow, then so will be his hypotheses. This narrow approach is continually revealed when people try to give an explanation of the facts, and squeeze them into a limited and pre-conceived view of how people behave. Such phrases as 'Of course, it was a woman driver' or 'He's very introverted, like all accountants' or 'Typical trade-union behaviour', are indicative of this approach and say more about the speaker than the situation they are trying to explain. The effective counsellor will keep an open mind, being neither surprised by what he hears nor afraid to go into areas which others may think are out of bounds.

SUMMARY

The effective counsellor helps his client explore and clarify his problems and find his own solutions. There are seven important aspects to successful counselling:

1. Listening

The kind of listening required by the counsellor is active rather than passive. This means not only encouraging the client to do most of the talking, but ensuring that he knows he is the centre of the counsellor's attention and interest.

2. Recognising the 'presenting problem'

The counsellor needs to recognise that the initial problem presented is rarely a full statement of the real problem. The client is likely to use a form of words which is generally acceptable and he will need encouragement from the counsellor to go further.

3. Finding the core problem

The core problem is the heart of the matter which is worrying the client. It always concerns his situation at the present time and usually involves his relationship with other people.

4. Recognising and admitting feelings

Effective counselling allows a person to explore and recognise the feelings associated with the problem.

5. Criticism

Criticism makes people feel threatened and they protect themselves by operating defence mechanisms. The result is that the counselling process stops, even though the interview may continue.

6. The problem-solving process

The counsellor should follow these stages as he helps the client deal with his problem:

   (a) Recognising the presenting problem
   (b) Finding the core problem
   (c) Discovering why it is a problem
   (d) Recognising and explaining feelings
   (e) Examining possible solutions and alternatives
   (f) Recognising their implications
   (g) Deciding on a course of action.

7. Influencing the direction

Even though the counsellor is trying not to lead his client down any pre-determined path, his every question and response will immediately give the conversation direction and emphasis. If he has a broad knowledge of human nature, his questions will direct the client towards greater self-understanding and an ability to select a course of action which is right for him.

4

Counselling and Performance Appraisal

Part of every manager's job must be to appraise the performance of his subordinates. This may happen after a particular assignment or project and, in many of the large auditing firms, for instance, a manager completes an assignment report for each person involved at the end of a particular audit. This is also happening more and more in computer software firms, where consultants are forming project teams to work with clients and the teams are appraised at the project's completion. But the most common method of appraisal is the Company Appraisal scheme where at regular intervals – usually once a year – the manager completes a performance assessment of his subordinates' work over the last period. Such an appraisal covers various aspects of work and may entail ticking boxes, marking five-point scales or simply writing an

open-ended report. As well as this, many companies operate some sort of 'management by objective' scheme and
use the targets that were agreed and set at the previous
meeting as the measure for the actual achievement.

Trying to work all of these schemes can cause immense
problems. Not least is the anxiety felt by managers when
they have to hold an appraisal interview with someone
who does not want it and with whom they have little
sympathy or empathy. Another problem is the actual
paper system. One sheet must go to the personnel department, one is retained by the manager, the subordinate is
given a copy – but only of certain things! It is not unusual
for the preparation and distribution of the paperwork to
take up to 90 per cent of everyone's effort in these schemes,
leaving only 10 per cent for the actual appraisal.

There can be only one way forward which is likely to
prove effective. *An appraisal scheme must be client-
centred.* That is, the primary task of appraisal must be to
help the subordinate, and anything that hinders this
should be modified or scrapped. Just as effective counselling requires a certain relationship, so an effective
appraisal scheme can only operate within an appropriate
organisational climate.

There are many reasons why organisations carry out
performance appraisal, for instance:

- to provide knowledge of individual performance
- to plan for future promotions and successions
- to assess training and development needs
- to provide information for salary planning and special
awards
- to contribute to corporate career planning and progression.

But the prime aim must be to help the person being
appraised. This means that he should know exactly where
he stands with his boss and within the company and can
take appropriate action to build on his strengths and
reduce his weaknesses. Not only is this in line with good
human relations, it also has the practical result of con-

tributing to the development of the organisation's most important asset – its people.

If the main purpose in appraising a person's performance is to contribute to their motivation and development, *appraisal must be linked with counselling.* If appraisal means evaluating an employee's worth, then counselling means communicating that information in such a way that the individual can use it positively. That being so, certain principles about an appraisal and counselling interview can be stated.

PRINCIPLES FOR AN APPRAISAL AND COUNSELLING INTERVIEW

1. Everything written should be shown and shared. This is probably the most important principle for the following reasons:

Secrecy breeds suspicion. Whilst the manager may feel he has good reason to keep certain facts or opinion hidden, his subordinate is bound to put the worst construction on this. Suspicion is the emotion most likely to destroy a counselling relationship. As well as this, it is vital for a subordinate to know the source of any criticism; nothing is more worrying than hearing one's boss say 'I gather that you have done so and so' without disclosing who has told him.

Elliott Jaques put this well:

This kind of behaviour is infuriating. It arouses feelings of contempt toward the manager for listening to tales from others, and scorn for the unknown others. Such reactions are not surprising since secret tale-bearing is a very paranoiagenic (fear-creating) act. Any organisation in which behaviour of this kind becomes rife is going to pieces: the behaviour is a powerful aid to the disintegration. *(A General Theory of Bureaucracy)*

There are frequently two aspects in appraisals which are
not communicated, and these relate to poor performance
and potential promotion.

With regard to poor performance, the secrecy reflects
the manager's own anxiety. How can he tell his subordinate that he is doing badly? The answer (which is easier
said than done) is that no-one can improve until they are
aware of their faults. And, of course, if this is dealt with in
a counselling manner, the manager himself may find that
he is part of the problem and so can become part of the
solution.

The usual argument for not communicating information regarding potential promotion to the subordinate is
that he will interpret it as a statement of fact and will be
very disappointed if it does not happen. On the other hand,
a person surely has a right to know how he is regarded by
his company and should also have plenty of time to consider a possible future promotion and the effect this may
have on him and his family. The manager must ensure
that the subordinate understands that the promotion is
not a certainty and that there are various factors which
might affect the final decision, especially the subordinate's continuing high performance.

How many companies have had the unhappy experience
of losing their best men because they were never told of
the company's high opinion of them?

Finally, if there is still something that the manager
feels he cannot communicate to his subordinate, then that
is probably a good enough reason for excluding it from the
appraisal report.

2. The appraisal report should be finalised in the presence
of the subordinate.

The main reason for this is that the subordinate should
know exactly what the completed document contains
before it goes on the file. The other reason is that if the
appraisal is communicated in a counselling interview,
new facts may arise which may alter the manager's view
and he may wish to change what he has already written.
The subordinate may also disagree with some parts of the

appraisal and if, at the end of the interview he still disagrees, he must have the opportunity to state his disagreement, which must be recorded.

A further point is that many schemes involve the subordinate's 'grandfather', i.e. the manager's manager, who will not necessarily see the subordinate, but will write a comment on the report, possibly following a discussion with the manager. Again, there seems no reason why the subordinate should not see these comments and he may even learn something from the views of a senior executive.

3. The subordinate should contribute a major part to the appraisal.

No-one knows the subordinate better than he knows himself, and in a counselling relationship with an encouraging manager, he can explore and assess his own performance. Self-appraisal is particularly effective in two areas. The first concerns the area of weak performance and in a supportive relationship individuals can be remarkably open and honest about themselves. The counselling manager enables his subordinate to examine these areas in an analytic rather than a critical way, and helps him discover courses of action which will lead to improvement. Where these facts have to be written into an appraisal report, the manager will choose words which demonstrate the subordinate's self-insight and which therefore do not become incriminating or damning. Rather, they reveal the qualities of self-knowledge and become positive factors in the overall appraisal.

The other effective area resulting from self-appraisal is career progression. Managers are likely to see a subordinate's future in terms of what has happened to other people in their department and, especially in terms of their own career progression. By giving his subordinate the opportunity to talk about his aspirations, he may well discover aims and ambitions of which he himself was totally unaware. This may enable him to plan work experience and specific training for the subordinate, or at least note these hopes on the appraisal report, so that central personnel are aware of them.

THE DYNAMICS OF AN APPRAISAL/COUN-SELLING INTERVIEW

Most managers and their subordinates feel apprehensive about taking part in an appraisal and counselling interview. Harold J. Leavitt has tried to explain this by dividing manager's styles into two major categories – 'direct' and 'relational'. 'Direct' styles are used by get-it-done, task-oriented people who compete to win. 'Relational' styles, in contrast are used by managers and always involve relationships with other people. They help, support and back up other people and often get their feelings of achievement by contributing to the success of others. Using these two concepts, Leavitt writes about performance appraisals:

> Performance appraisal systems offer a clear example of direct/relational dilemma of modern management. Almost every organisation uses some form of comparative performance evaluation scheme. But the words 'comparative' and 'performance' and 'evaluation' are all direct-style words. Extreme relational-type managers don't like to be compared or evaluated or to have their performance measured. They prefer to 'accept' and 'support' and 'help' one another. The very concept of individual performance evaluation presumes individuals competing with one another to achieve individual rewards. That may be why both managers and managed are so universally uncomfortable with performance evaluation procedures. They violate our relational side. The best that such evaluation schemes engender is a love-hate ambivalence. Performance appraisal programmes don't founder because they use the wrong forms or the wrong categories; they get into trouble because both honest appraisers and realistic appraisees hate to confront what is almost inevitably an uncomfortable – indeed unhuman – evaluation interview. So they either skip it or muck it up. (*Organizational Dynamics*)

It is useful to analyse some of the emotional factors

which may be present on both sides at such an interview and which will affect the meeting to a greater or lesser extent.

The manager – positive feelings

To be helpful and understanding By virtue of his greater experience and superior position in the organisation, the manager may be justified in feeling that he has knowledge and understanding which will help his subordinate. He may also feel that he has a good understanding of people's behaviour, learnt both from his working experience and some theoretical knowledge of the behavioural sciences. The danger here is that the manager, seeing his subordinate encounter problems similar to those he himself has experienced, will offer solutions which worked for him. To be helpful and understanding in a positive way, the manager must recognise that his subordinate is an autonomous human being with a complex and unique personality, and that his problems require their own, individual solutions.

To be kind and tolerant Most managers would like to see themselves as kind and tolerant – the sort of boss who is liked and respected by his staff. However, this should not lead to a policy of appeasement: the manager who is frightened to point out the truth so colludes with his subordinate's poor performance or fantasy. Feelings of kindness are used positively when the manager helps the subordinate to see the facts of the situation and to come to grips with reality.

For instance, for a manager to allow a subordinate to continue to think that his performance is good and that promotion and salary increases will come in the future, when he knows full well that this is unlikely, is not an act of kindness. Neither is it kind, as occasionally happens, for the manager to withhold knowledge of future promotion, giving the subordinate a surprise at the last minute like an unexpected present. In this case, the subordinate is helped by knowing of the promotion as soon as possible so that he has time to make the necessary adjustments, both physical and psychological.

The manager – negative feelings

Fear of the interview itself. The thought of carrying out an appraisal and counselling interview can make a manager very anxious and these anxieties are based on a variety of fears. The first fear concerns the interview itself – will he do it well? Will his subordinate see him as a fool, unable to cope with the situation and letting it get out of hand, with unforeseen results? Does he understand the actual purpose of the appraisal scheme? What will happen if the subordinate asks him questions to which he doesn't know the answer? All these fears are an inevitable part of counselling and are part of the price a manager pays for trying to build effective relationships with his subordinates. They can only be diminished by practice and the more interviews a manager carries out, the less these fears will hinder him.

Counselling training, where people have an opportunity to practise facing up to these fears and overcoming them, is very useful.

Fear of unleashing powerful emotions. Because performance appraisal is such a personal activity, the manager may fear that the subordinate has extremely strong feelings concerning his work and concerning his boss. He may fear that one inappropriate word will unleash a whole range of emotions which would be highly embarrassing and difficult to control. However, whilst the subordinate may have strong feelings, it is rare for emotions to come bursting out like lava from a volcano. The opposite is more usual, that is, people are reticent about their feelings and usually need a lot of encouragement before they will express them. The way to reduce this fear is to build up a relationship with the subordinate in which the expression of feelings plays a natural part.

Envying the subordinate. Envy can be described as 'the angry feeling that another person possesses and enjoys something desirable – the envious impulse being to take it away or spoil it' (M. Klein, 1957). On the face of it, the manager has little reason to envy his subordinate. After all, he has a higher position, a larger salary, etc. But there may be other things he envies – such as his youth and health and the greater opportunities he seems to have for future success and achievement.

Perhaps the most common cause for envy lies in the subordinate's qualifications. Many managers who are not graduates, but who hold responsible posts, are deeply envious of graduates and consequently look for ways to devalue them – 'bloody graduates, they think the world owes them a living'. Or as an engineering director once said, 'No graduate's any use to me until he's worn a pair of overalls and got his hands dirty!'

Envy can also lead a manager to hinder his subordinates efforts to prevent him succeeding; or else to belittle any success he does have. The more the manager can acknowledge to himself that he has these feelings, the more he can control them and minimise their negative effect.

The subordinate – positive feelings

To be liked and accepted. One of the most basic desires in everyone is to be liked, and even loved, and accepted for what one is, warts and all. Because of the very nature of their relationship, the subordinate places a special value on the boss's estimation of him. Whilst this is a natural feeling, it can lead to overdependence and to a desire to please at any cost. In appraising and counselling, the interview can sometimes be used by a subordinate as a confessional, and he waits to hear the words of absolution. If the boss colludes in such fantasies, the subordinate is encouraged in his feelings of dependence and may even say such things as 'Tell me what to do. I'll accept your opinion. After all, you're the boss!' An overriding wish to be liked, leads the subordinate to deny the awkward and difficult parts of his nature. But although they might cause friction, it is better that they should be faced, than be sacrificed on the altar of his boss's affection.

To get help with problems. It has been stressed that good counselling helps a person solve his own problems. A manager can also give his subordinate support and sympathy. Of course, not every appraisal interview will require this sort of approach, and many subordinates will have no serious problems at work or at home. However, if a counselling relationship exists, the subordinate knows that his boss is interested in him, and will listen to him because he really cares. The interveue can then fulfill a need which might otherwise not be met.

The subordinate – negative feelings

Fear of criticism and punishment. An appraisal interview aims to evaluate all areas of performance, both strong and weak, successes and failures. The greatest fear in the mind of any subordinate at an appraisal interview is that his performance will be criticised and, like a prisoner in the dock, he will be found guilty. The fear of criticism is linked to the wish to be liked by the boss, and concern for salary and career; there may even be a fear of being sacked. Whilst legislation now prevents unlawful dismissal, there is no doubt that a manager can affect his subordinate's future in all sorts of ways and make his daily life extremely unpleasant. The only way in which these fears can be allayed is by building a relationship between manager and subordinate in which poor performance is discussed as it happens and the manager shows himself to be fair and trustworthy in his day-to-day behaviour.

SUMMARY

A. Every manager has to appraise the performance of his subordinates and this usually involves a formal interview. Company appraisal schemes can be very time-consuming and if they are to be useful, they must be client-centred. This means that appraisal interviews must be linked with counselling, so that the subordinate can use the appraisal information positively. An appraisal and counselling interview is more likely to be effective if the following points are borne in mind.

1. The manager should show his subordinate everything that he has written about him and share it with him. Anything else breeds suspicion. This is especially true of poor performance, and it is the only way in which improvements are likely to be made.

2. The appraisal report should be finalised in the presence of the subordinate. This allows him to know exactly what is being placed on file and provides him with the opportunity, if he wishes, to record any disagreement he may have with the report.

3. The subordinate should contribute a large part of the appraisal. Self-appraisal is particularly effective in two areas:

(a) Poor performance. In a counselling relationship people can exercise self-criticism, which is a prerequisite of change and improvement.

(b) Career progression. Self-appraisal allows a person to explore his career aspirations so that appropriate training and work experience can be planned, to the benefit of the individual and the organisation.

B. Both manager and subordinate can feel anxious and apprehensive about an appraisal interview. An analysis of the emotional dynamics in these situations can help both parties to understand the reasons for this and to cope better.

1. The manager's positive feelings.

(a) The manager wants to be helpful and under-standing, but may be inclined to offer advice too closely related to his own experience. He will offer positive help when he recognises his subordinate as a unique indi-vidual.

(b) He wants to be kind and tolerant and to be liked by his staff. But he must not let these feelings prevent him from pointing out the reality of the situation, even if this is painful.

2. The manager's negative feelings.

(a) The manager may be fearful of the interview itself and worry that he will make a mess of it. This is the price he pays for building a strong relationship with his subordinates and these fears will diminish with practice.

(b) He may fear that the interview will get very emotional and that the subordinate may express strong hostile feeling towards him. These fears can be reduced by developing a relationship with his subordinate in which the expression of feelings is a normal part of that relationship.

(c) The manager may have feelings of envy towards his subordinate concerning his youth, health, qualifications or career opportunities. He needs to ack-nowledge these and not let them influence his behaviour by belittling or hindering his subordinate's progress and achievements.

3. The subordinate's positive feelings.

(a) The subordinate wants to be liked by his boss and receive his approbation. But he must not let this desire lead him to deny the awkward parts of himself and take up a dependent attitude.

(b) The wish to get help with any problems he has can, with a counselling relationship, become a realistic part of the interview.

4.The subordinate's negative feelings.

The most likely emotion which the subordinate will feel is fear of being criticised for his work or behaviour, and unless this fear is allayed, the interview will achieve nothing. Only the manager can do this through a counselling relationship which shows that he is fair and trustworthy.

REFERENCES

Jaques, E., *A General Theory of Bureaucracy,* Heinemann, 1976

Klein, M., *Envy and Gratitude,* Tavistock Publications, 1957, p.6

Leavitt, H. J. and Lipman-Brown, J., 'A Case for the Relational Manager,' *Organizational Dynamics,* Summer, 1980

5

Improving Transactions

Counselling is very much to do with the ways in which people relate and behave with one another. The important relationship within which counselling takes place has been characterised by such words as 'encouragement', 'trust' and 'openness'. No doubt every manager and subordinate would like to have this kind of relationship. However, business pressures and personality conflicts can all work against this ideal. There is often mistrust and suspicion between people, resulting in criticism and fear which can make counselling difficult if not impossible; neither party plans it that way, but the same fraught situations occur time and time again, leading to rows and bad feelings.

An analysis of the mechanisms that operate when people try to communicate their thoughts and feelings to each other may be helpful.

There are many theories put forward by psychologists to explain these matters, and all have their followers, but few managers have the time or inclination to study such writers as Freud or Jung. Recently, however, a method of analysing behaviour has been developed which has the virtues of being simple and easily communicated. This is called 'Transactional Analysis' and was developed by the late Eric Berne, author of the bestselling book *Games People Play*. Transactional Analysis has something very specific to say about effective counselling (although its aims are far wider than this), and many managers have found the theory easy to absorb and to relate to their own experience. It is therefore described below in some detail.

EGO-STATES

It is common experience that the same person can behave very differently at different times. A person who is rational and able to consider calmly all the aspects of a problem may, on occasion, become angry and highly emotional. A person may behave quite differently at home and at work. When these changes in behaviour are extreme, it may even be commented that 'he seemed to be a different person'.

Transactional Analysis explains this by saying that everyone is always in one of three possible 'ego-states'. 'Ego-state' simply means 'the state I am in' and includes the language and tone of voice we use, the emotions and feelings we have and our physical appearance and stance. The three ego-states are called Parent, Adult and Child and we move from one to the other continuously as we react to the different situations in which we find ourselves.

Parent

The Parent ego-state contains all the values and morals
we have been taught since birth. It contains our standards
for living and enables us to say what is right or wrong;
what is good or bad. These values come from our actual
parents: they were the chief influence on our behaviour
and their words and actions moulded our early years.
Their words and attitudes are permanently stored in our
minds and can be switched on rather like a tape recorder.
The stern look, the wagging finger, the use of such words
as 'Never let me catch you doing that again!' all indicate
that someone is in their Parent ego-state. But our parents
were loving and nurturing as well as critical, and this side
of our experience is also present in the Parent ego-state,
showing itself in caring and comforting behaviour and
such words as 'Don't worry, I'll take care of it'.

Here are some characteristics of the Parent ego-state:

Words   Don't, never, always, well done, splendid
Voice   Stern, critical, angry, comforting, concerned
Gestures   Frown, wag finger, arm around shoulder
Attitude   Authoritarian, judgemental, caring

Adult

The Adult ego-state is the rational, unemotional way
we have of behaving which deals with the reality of
what is actually happening. It contains all the information, knowledge and skills we have accumulated and
can deal with facts and figures, solve problems, consider
different courses of action and compute their possible
outcomes and implications. Because of this, the Adult is
the state in which we learn and in which we can choose
to take new and different approaches.

Some characteristics of the Adult ego-state are:

Words   How? What? Why? When? Is it practical?
Voice   Calm, even
Gestures   Alert, thoughtful
Attitude   Analytic, evaluative, attentive, constructive

Child

The Child ego-state contains all the emotions and feelings as they were experienced in childhood. At birth, all we have is our Child, laughing or crying, and this Natural Child is still a part of ourselves, self-centred and demanding, spontaneous and uninhibited, loving and fun-loving. However, this Natural Child is rapidly affected by the attitudes of parents and other influential people in the process of socialisation, resulting in the Adapted Child. The Adapted Child results from the rewards and punishments given by the parents as, for instance, the infant learns that it is more likely to get what it wants by asking politely rather than screaming for it.

Here are some characteristics of the Child ego-state:

Words Want, can't, wish, hope, please, thank you, I wonder . . ., wouldn't it be nice if . . .
Voice Giggling, whining, excited, whispering, pleading
Gestures Spontaneous, sad, happy, whimsical
Attitude Joking, ashamed, creative, manipulative, sulky, curious, dependent, scared

All three ego-states are vital to effective living and none is 'better' than the other. The important things to realise is that in communicating with other people, each state brings different results and has important implications for work and relationships. This way of looking at behaviour is called Transactional Analysis, and based on these ideas a person can be represented by three circles in the following way:

Basically, when we are in the Parent – we believe; when we are in the Adult – we think; and when we are in the Child – we feel.

This simple model of behaviour provides a useful way of analysing any transaction which takes place between people. Anyone starting a conversation must be speaking from either their Parent, Adult or Child ego-state and the other person's reply must also come from one of these.

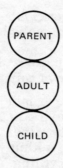

Here is a simple example:

Manager: Don't ever let me catch you writing a report like this again. It's a load of rubbish!
Subordinate: I'm very sorry, I only had two days to finish it. But it won't happen again.

Clearly, the manager is in the Parent ego-state criticising the report in very general terms, and treating his subordinate like a naughty boy.

The subordinate, not unnaturally, replies from his Child ego-state and, because he feels guilty, apologises and promises to do better in the future, just as a small boy might respond to an angry father.

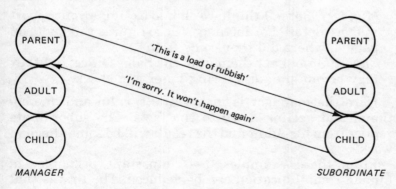

However, in the same situation, the exchange might be as follows:

Manager: John, the boss is playing hell over that report

and I'm scared we'll get clobbered. Could you re-write
bits of it, just enough to make him happy? I'm up to my
eyes in work.
Subordinate: Don't you worry, I'll take care of it. What
you want is a nice cup of coffee.

In this case, the manager is in his Child, frightened of
his boss's anger and behaving in a very dependent way on
his subordinate. The subordinate responds from his Parent, comforting him like a kindly father, indicating that
he will take care of everything.

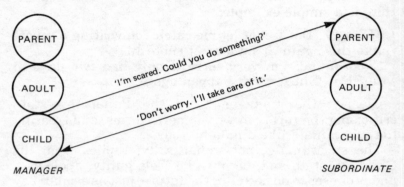

Or, the exchange might be:

Manager: John, I think we should examine your report
in more detail. For instance, those figures you quote on
page 3, where did they come from?
Subordinate: I got them from the Sales Office, but they
may be out of date. I'll ring Peter and check.

Here the manager is in his Adult, calm and unemotional and getting down to the facts. The subordinate
replies from his Adult and the result will be some effecitve
work.

From these examples, two important principles of
human communication can be deduced. The first is that
the person who begins speaking and initiates the transaction is (unconsciously) trying to 'hook' the complementary
ego-state of the other. In the first example above, the
manager in his critical Parent hooks the guilty Child of

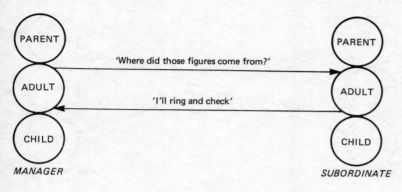

his subordinate. In the second example, the manager in his dependent and scared Child hooks the comforting Parent of the subordinate. In the final example, the calm, problem-solving Adult of the manager connects with the Adult of the subordinate. As we shall see, not every transaction is complementary, but many transactions involve Parent-Child ego-states or else they are Adult-Adult.

The second principle is that in these kinds of complementary transactions the communication can go on indefinitely, although the quality of the conversation may not be high. For instance, many managers have a Parent-Child relationship with their subordinates and they both work comfortably in these ego-states over many years.

Of course, life at work (or at home) is never a series of smooth transactions. People get angry or upset, rows occur and relationships get damaged. It is in this area of bad communications that TA can provide an analytical tool to explain what is happening. Put simply, communications stop and bad situations arise when the transactions cut across each other. Here is a classic work situation to illustrate this:

Manager: (threateningly) You're responsible for getting these budgets. If anything goes wrong, I'll hold you responsible! (Parent)
Subordinate: How dare you speak to me like that. Apologise at once! (Parent)

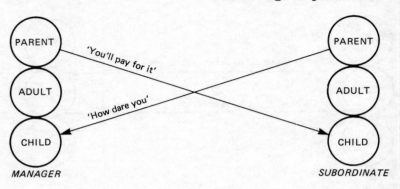

Both people are in their Parent, one angry and threatening, the other equally angry and full of righteous indignation. Each is treating the other like a child and so their transactions cross each other. The scene is all set for a really good row.

Here is another example of crossed transactions:

Secretary: Please help me find that letter from Head Office. If I've lost it the boss will kill me!
Colleague: Don't blame me. I haven't got it.

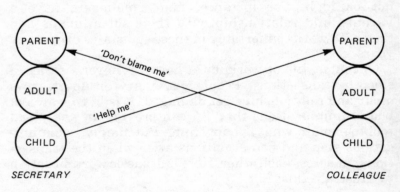

In this instance, the secretary is in her Child, but her friend also replies from her Child and so the transactions are crossed.

Just reading these examples one can imagine the tensions that inevitably result from these exchanges and the 'atmosphere' that is created and remains possibly for some time.

To summarise so far, TA provides a unique and simple way to analyse and understand what happens when two people are having a conversation and exchanging views. Two important points emerge.

Firstly, in every conversation we have, there are always three options available. We can start or respond from either our Parent, Adult or Child and the results will be different in each case. Because of the behavioural patterns we have all established over a number of years, many of our reactions have become automatic and seem inevitable. For instance, if a subordinate makes a mistake it may seem the natural thing for the manager to reprimand him and behave in the Critical Parent. Likewise, if we are criticised, we usually apologise and make our excuses (from the Child) or else start a fight (from the Parent). But these ideas from TA show that this is neither inevitable nor desirable. It is the realisation of these potential choices with the resulting increase in personal freedom that makes TA so stimulating and effective.

The second point is that poor relationships, rows and unpleasant feelings between people can usually be explained by analysing the conversations that take place and seeing where, in TA terms, the lines cross. Understanding this does not immediately result in sweetness and light, but it does mean that on the next occasion, a different approach can be considered, which may prove to be more effective and constructive.

WORKING IN THE ADULT

It should now be obvious that effective counselling will only occur when both manager and subordinate are operating in their Adult ego-state. This is not to deny the importance of either the Parent or the Child. But the Adult is the appropriate and necessary condition for doing counselling work. When we operate from the Adult we behave as rational, unemotional people, in touch with reality and acting in an alert and thoughtful manner. Consider, as an example, the following statement made by a subordinate at an appraisal and counselling interview:

> What really concerns me is my future prospects. I'm 51, a departmental manager and I've been in this position for the last six years, before you became my boss. I do my job efficiently, but I ought to get promotion soon if I'm going to make the grade. I'd like to ask you straight out – when will I get promotion?

This kind of statement puts any manager in a very delicate situation and there are a variety of ways in which he can answer. Here are some possible responses, based on the different ego-states he may be in:

A. *Critical Parent*
You know very well that these decisions are made by the central personnel department. The more you keep on about it the less you are helping yourself. What you've got to do is show me, over the next six months that you're capable of being promoted. That cock-up you made last week didn't exactly inspire me with confidence.

B. *Nurturing Parent*
Look Fred, you've nothing to worry about. You know I take care of all the boys in my department. When have I ever let you down? I'll put in a good word for you in the right place, never fear. Meanwhile, keep your chin up and things will come right in the end. After all, like my old father used to say – it will all be the same in 100 years!

C. *Child*
How should I know? Nobody tells me anything around here. They must think I've nothing better to do than to spend all my time on staff matters. It's not fair. I wish personnel would get up off its backside and do some work for a change. Why don't you go and ask them? Not

that you'll get a decision out of that lot. But I don't know
why you're worried. Look at me! I'm five years older
than you and I don't know whay they're planning for
me. And the wife's not all that well.

Each of these responses would cause a different reaction
in the subordinate. To response A, the subordinate is
likely to feel sad and depressed and worried that in some
undefined way his performance is below standard.
Because the criticism is so vague, he has nothing specific
to work on other than the comment about the incident last
week. He may well latch on to this and respond with a
string of excuses (Child) or try and start a fight (Parent).

The subordinate may feel a little comforted and reas-
sured by the friendly words of the manager who gives
response B. But he will recognise that what is being said is
'flannel', a smokescreen of words that are easily said but
which on analysis, mean absolutely nothing. They may
sell serve the manager's purpose, which is to move on
quickly from this embarrassing situation. Unless the subordinate has a great deal of courage and determination, he
will accept the reassurance and agree with the manager's
words. But, of course, nothing has changed and he will
leave the interview with his problems and worries unresolved.

If the manager gives response C, the subordinate is
likely to feel confused and baffled. After all, if his boss
apparently doesn't know about his own future, how can he
possibly counsel and advise his subordinate? They
apparently have a common enemy in the personnel
department and the outcome could be a game called 'Ain't
it Awful'. However, the manager has signalled loudly that
he is in his Child by the way he refers to his sick wife. The
most likely outcome is that the subordinate will respond
with sympathy, hoping the wife will soon be better, and so
on, i.e. moving into the Nurturing Parent.

These three responses have one thing in common: they
all prevent effective counselling. They are all likely to
engage the subordinate's Parent or Child so that the work
of analysing and resolving his problem is made impos-

sible. It could be argued that this is in fact the manager's motive, because it enables him to avoid facing up to a delicate issue.

The manager's *Adult* responses could be something like this:

> I understand your concern, Fred. Looking back over your time in this department, can you think of any reasons why you may have been overlooked for promotion?
>
> *OR*
>
> To be honest with you, I'm not sure. You see, when I put in my reports recommending promotions, I must be fair to the other people in our department. Take John and Terry for instance. They've both got full membership of the institute and I know you're only an associate member. That makes very little difference in your present position but I think it must be taken into account for higher level work. Are you unhappy in your job? You seem to run your department well. Perhaps you're feeling a bit stale?
>
> *OR*
>
> I'm interested to know why you want promotion so badly. You run your department well and you're at the top of your salary scale. Promotion won't give you that much extra, especially after tax. What are the advantages you hope to get?

The reader can no doubt think up a great number of other Adult responses, and each will have the same effect. Because they are in the Adult and ask a question, they are most likely to get an Adult response from the subordinate. The result is that he will be enabled to analyse his own problem further and gain more self-insight. In the above case, the solution appears to be a realisation of the fact that he will not get promotion and an understanding of the reasons why. If the counselling manager can facilitate this recognition and self-acceptance in his subordinate, then he will have provided real help.

CONCLUSION

No one can begin to solve his problems until he is able to face up to the realities of his situation. This essential and sometimes painful process can only come about when the individual is in his Adult, realising all the facts and their implications and as a result deciding on some appropriate course of action. The effective counsellor facilitates this process by being himself in his Adult and asking questions which allow the subordinate to explore his own world. The outcome is not only the resolution of the problem, but also a person who is developing greater self-insight and who is growing psychologically.

SUMMARY

Effective counselling requires an open and trusting relationship between the counsellor and his client. However,
pressures at work can cause hostility and suspicion between a manager and his subordinate which makes counselling extremely difficult. Transactional Analysis provides a way of understanding the mechanisms of interpersonal communication and suggests ways of behaviour
which are likely to be beneficial for counselling.

A. People are always in one of three ego-states: Parent,
Adult or Child.

Parent — The Parent ego-state consists of the values
and morals we received from our parents. It is the state
in which we are critical and judgemental, typified by
the wagging finger and the stern rebuke. It is also the
state in which, like our parents, we can be loving and
nurturing, taking care of people.
Adult — In the Adult ego-state, we are unemotional,
dealing rationally with the facts that concern us. We
use all the information, knowledge and skills we possess, and this is the appropriate state for learning and
problem-solving.
Child — In the Child ego-state we experience all the
emotions and feelings as they were experienced in
childhood. These feelings typically involve sadness, fun,
rebelliousness, creativity, fear and dependency.

All three states are part of normal behaviour; the skill lies
in choosing the state which is appropriate to the situation.

B. In any conversation, each person is speaking and
responding from one of their three ego-states. As long as
these transactions are complementary, i.e. Parent-
Parent, Parent-Child, Adult-Adult, Child-Child or
Child-Parent, communication can proceed smoothly. But
communication breaks down when the transactions cross,

and this is usually when both persons speak from their Parent and direct their words to the other's Child.

C. Using Transactional Analysis theory, it becomes obvious that effective counselling will only happen when both the counsellor and his client are working in their Adult ego-state. The Adult enables both parties to look at the facts of the situation and rationally examine possible solutions and their implications. It also allows the client to choose new courses of action and new ways of behaviour, resulting in learning and growth.

REFERENCES

Berne, E., *Games People Play,* Grove Press Inc., 1964; Penguin Books, 1968.

6

Journey Into Life-Space

Counselling is a very private and personal activity. It usually concerns only two people, both of whom are trying to come to grips with reality. The counsellor is concerned with the reality of the person he is attempting to help as well as the problem which he presents. Who is he? How does he think? What sort of a person is he?

The better the counsellor can recognise and accept the fact that the person he is dealing with is different from anybody else in the world, the more genuine help he will bring to the situation. But this can also be threatening because meeting strangers can create anxiety, and the recognition that someone is different from ourselves can be frightening.

To overcome these fears and anxieties and to avoid the hard work of getting to know someone, there is a tendency to put labels on people and then to start dealing with the label – not the person.

The labels we use come from powerful memories of past experiences. For instance, our early family lives are bound to be strong in our memories and especially the roles of our parents. It is likely therefore that many managers who are middle-aged tend to see their younger subordinates as their children and treat them accordingly. This is not always done consciously, but when counselling, the handiest label to put on the subordinate is 'son' or 'daughter', and the manager then proceeds to play the wise patriarch or the stern father. However, if he wishes to play the part of counsellor, he must throw away the 'child' label and attempt to meet the real person who is confronting him. (This can be a two-way process: the subordinate may come to a counselling meeting with the expectation of meeting a father-figure.)

Other labels we use may be based on myth and folklore concerning people's appearance. Eyes too close together indicate untrustworthiness or even, in some people's mind, criminality. Eyebrows that meet in the middle are a sign of temper – as is red hair. A straight nose indicates honesty, and so on. I even heard someone describe a candidate after an interview as 'having the long upper lip of the humorist!'

As well as individual features, a person's general appearance can sometimes remind us of someone else and this may affect the way we behave to the new person.

All of these labelling techniques are part of normal behaviour and providing the counsellor is aware of them, they should not hinder effective counselling.

But one technique of labelling which can be detrimental to counselling is that of stereotyping. This can happen particularly at work when certain functions are thought to attract similar personalities. Perhaps accountants and finance people are most likely to be stereotyped – 'They're all the same. Narrow minded, unimaginative, work to the rules, and are cold and aloof'. Sales people are often labelled as hearty extroverts who fiddle their expenses, enjoy a lunchtime drink and play golf every Friday. This kind of labelling can simply be a bit of fun, just as stereotyping the Welsh or the English, the Germans or the French has its place in good-humoured banter. But it is more serious when people are only allowed to play the stereotype. For instance, in a meeting, an accountant might have something to say about the people-side of the business but his view may be completely discounted – 'After all, he's only the accountant.' Similarly, academics may be stereotyped as ineffective people, living in an ivory tower and not in the real world, who are more at home with books than with people.

As has been said, this process of labelling is something that everyone does to avoid the hard work of really getting to know an individual. In many circumstances it may not matter very much, although in its extreme forms it can be highly dangerous, resulting in racial prejudice and the irrational dislike of large groups of people and even nations.

But for the counsellor, any labelling leads to ineffectiveness. His job, as far as possible is to free his mind from any comparisons he may be tempted to make, and to recognise the uniqueness of the person he is meeting, as if this was the first person he has ever met. With this attitude, counselling can become a genuine encounter where fresh attitudes and new beginnings can emerge and where change becomes a real possibility – for both parties.

Counselling involves an encounter. For the counsellor, this means trying to enter the private and personal world of the other person in order to be of help. One way of describing this is to use the idea of 'life-space'.

LIFE-SPACE

The concept of 'life-space' was first put forward by the great psychologist, Kurt Lewin. He was trying to show how all behaviour is based in the present moment or, in the phrase he coined, 'the here and now'. He illustrated

this with the diagram below, representing the life space of
a child.

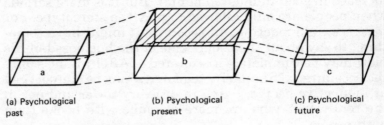

(a) Psychological   (b) Psychological   (c) Psychological
past   present   future

Life space of a child (Based on Lewin)

Life-space of a child

This diagram represents a child's life-space at the present
time. The child has a large part of this space concerned
with what is actually happening now, including all his
feelings and emotions (the 'psychological present'). But
his behaviour is also affected by his past experiences,
although for a child, this is relatively short (the
'psychological past'). At the same time, his present situation is also affected by his hopes, fears and expectations of
what the future may hold (the 'psychological future'). Any
action which the child now takes is in some way affected
by these three aspects of his life-space.

The adult equally has a 'life-space' but it is different
from that of the child because of the greater psychological
time perspectives. As the diagram shows, the adult, in
contrast to the child, has not only a longer past available
for recall, but is also able to imagine a more distant future.

In other words, every individual exists in a psychological field of forces which, for him, determines and limits
his behaviour. This 'force-field' is another idea of Lewin's
and is based on theories from physics, which refer to mag-
netism and electricity. For instance, the space around a
magnet is called a magnetic field and consists of invisible
lines of force. This is easily proved by placing a sheet of
paper over a magnet and then sprinkling iron filings on to
the paper. The filings immediately take up a particular

pattern, revealing the magnetic field. More importantly, it is the interaction of these force-fields, which result in the output of electric motors and generators.

The analogy to human behaviour is clear. Every individual has a psychological force-field around him which determines and limits his behaviour, and that is what Lewin called the 'life-space'. When one or more persons meet, their fields of force interact and the result is shown in their actual behaviour.

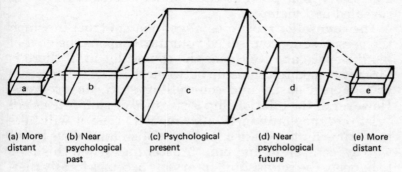

| (a) More distant | (b) Near psychological past | (c) Psychological present | (d) Near psychological future | (e) More distant |

Life space of an adult (Based on Lewin)

LIFE-SPACE AND COUNSELLING

When these ideas are used in relation to counselling, they illuminate the counselling process and point to effective ways of operating.

1. Entering the life-space

It becomes clear that the first thing the counsellor must do is to gain entry into the life-space of the person being counselled. Short of psychological violence, there is no way in which such an entry can be forced. The door into another's private world is a barrier to be removed. Just as everyone develops physical ways of defending themselves

from unwanted intruders, so people develop psychological defences which prevent their inner selves from being revealed and violated.

The counsellor must create a climate of trust in which the person being counselled voluntarily opens the door of his life-space and welcomes the counsellor in. If there is already a good relationship between the two, this process will happen easily and counselling starts to progress. However, if the relationship is strained or simply does not exist (i.e. they only meet infrequently) then it will take more time for the counsellor to establish himself as trustworthy, competent and non-threatening. When this fails to happen, the counselling interview becomes totally ineffective. The counsellor makes no connection with the other person who puts all his energy into defending his inner life from a possible attack.

2. Behaviour within the life space

Having access to an individual's private world is a privilege, and the counsellor, once he is invited into the other person's life-space, must respect this confidence. This is why criticism is so damaging to the counselling process. Criticism is essentially judging someone against one's own standards and pronouncing that their behaviour or performance is below these standards. This is an abuse of the counselling situation and offends against the autonomy of the individual. When it is done in the name of performance improvement and from the power position of superior to subordinate, it is even more objectionable.

Criticism will also inevitably stop the counselling process. Feeling criticised means feeling threatened and anyone who feels threatened when counselled immediately ejects the counsellor from their life-space. This can be compared with a visitor who is welcomed into a house and made at home, but who then starts to criticise the furniture or the decorations. Such a person will be asked to leave as soon as possible, and rightly so.

3. Exploring the life-space

The counsellor's role is to focus on the other person in order that he may be helped to focus on his problem. For the counsellor, this means that having gained the person's confidence, he can help him explore his life-space. This might seem a strange thing to suggest, for it could be argued that everyone knows themselves and does not require a tour of self-discovery. But the counsellor can help in three particular ways.

Firstly, people tend to push unpleasant facts and memories to the back of their mind and then do their best to forget about them. A skilled counsellor can help someone to 'remember' things which they would sooner forget but which may have a bearing on the current problem.

Secondly, the counsellor can help the person to see things from a different angle, just as an unusual camera shot can give new insights into a well known object.

Thirdly, the counsellor can help the person to consider possible outcomes and implications of certain courses of action. This might be done by asking the question 'What do you think will happen if you do so and so?' To which the answer may well be, 'I never thought of that!' Perhaps that is the skill of the counsellor in a nutshell: to get a person to consider an aspect of the problem which they would not otherwise have done.

4. Dealing with emotions and feelings

The life-space of an individual is, by definition, highly subjective, dealing with the world as that person experiences it. But the world is experienced not only in terms of facts and events but also in terms of emotions and feelings. (Someone has said that at any time we feel sad, mad, glad or bad!) Any problem brought for counselling will have feelings associated with it and these may be weak or strong. Sometimes the main component of the problem is an emotion such as strong feelings of love or anger towards someone which cannot be expressed. Some people are closely in touch with their feelings and can express them openly and clearly. Others appear to be dissociated from their feelings, and are not able to express them or appear not to know that they have any. Many people find it difficult to show their feelings, perhaps because as children they were discouraged from doing so. In effective counselling, the counsellor provides the opportunity for the person to express their feelings, and this often helps both parties to focus on the important issues. Any problem causes feelings, such as anxiety, worry, fear or apprehension, and the stronger they are felt the greater must be the problem. People generally welcome and value the opportunity to talk about their feelings and a simple question like 'How does that make you feel?' is often sufficient. There is a side-benefit in that the expression of feelings, especially if they have been bottled-up for a long time, brings genuine relief and can have a strongly therapeutic effect.

5. The life-space, reality and fantasy

A person's life-space is the world as that individual sees it. However, each person exists in the real world and must be able to react with and respond to the other 'realities' of people and events outside themselves. But because the reality of the external world may be harsh, everyone finds ways to minimise this harshness by fantasies, in which they indulge privately in the game of 'let's pretend'. (Kurt Lewin gave this aspect of the life-space the interesting name of 'irreality'.)

People use fantasy in a variety of ways. For instance, the facts of a past event may be re-arranged so that the person, in relating a particular incident, appears to have a more important role in what happened. Or else it may be that the re-arrangement allows the person to be blameless. This is frequently demonstrated by people describing a road accident: it is always the other person's fault. This is different from lying: it represents what the person wishes had happened.

Some people act on fantasies of what the future will be, based on a selective arrangement of the facts. For instance, a man may come to believe that he is bound to be promoted when his superior retires and he may tell his wife and friends that it is a fact. He may even increase his spending on the basis of this belief. Of course, when he fails to get promotion, the reality of the situation will cause him a great deal of unhappiness.

Perhaps the most common area of fantasy is that of self-perception. How do I see myself? Am I brilliant, capable and successful or else a failure and incompetent? There can be no 'right' answer to these questions, because they are internal questions and people swing from optimism to pessimism.

Everybody has fantasies and no doubt they contribute to living a healthy and enjoyable life. Perhaps one sign of 'abnormality' is when someone is dominated by their fantasies to such an extent that they lose touch with reality. It is the counsellor's job to see that discussion of the problem and any solutions offered are based on fact. This means ensuring that the client understands what has really happened in the past to cause the problem and realises the implications of the solutions he is considering. The more that the client can examine the actual situation, the more likely he is to discover his own realistic solutions. Ineffective counselling results when the counsellor fails to challenge a fantasy ('Are you sure that's true?') or actually colludes with it.

SOLUTIONS THAT FIT THE LIFE-SPACE

Because life-space is unique to each individual person, any solution to a problem must be tailor-made to fit that space. This is why other people's suggestions are usually discarded or, when accepted, frequently turn out to be inappropriate or even disastrous. Such suggestions are based on another viewpoint and different experience; the words that every counsellor should avoid are 'if I were you'. The appropriate and realistic solution must fit into the overall behaviour pattern of the individual and be congruent with his personality. This is why the counsellor should at all times be considerate of the other person's feelings and realise that any direct advice or guidance demanding a change of long-held beliefs is likely to be rejected.

ON LEAVING THE LIFE-SPACE

Bringing a counselling interview to an end requires as much skill as starting one. If the interview has been effective and the counsellor has entered the other person's life-space, then he must withdraw at the right time and in the right way. With regard to the timing, all managers are busy people and will have set aside a fixed period of time for the counselling session, usually not less than half an hour and not more than one hour. Having a fixed time is important because it puts a creative pressure on both people to get on with things, and enables things to be said at appropriate times. For instance, some things will only be said near the end of an interview, rather than at the beginning. It also means that the counsellor can structure his questions and approach to the time available, so that the end of his counselling work coincides with the end of the time period. When this does not happen, one or both parties leave the interview wishing that they had had more time.

With regard to withdrawal, this should be done in such
a way that the client feels satisified with the counselling
and is left with a personal piece of work to do. He should
not feel complacent, but should feel rather that real help
has been received and that something important and useful has been achieved.

SUMMARY

A. If a piece of counselling is to be effective, the counsellor must see his client as he really is, a unique individual, different from anyone else. But differences between people can be the cause of anxiety and fear, and it is easier to categorise people and deal with the label rather than the person. This can result in stereotyping, when, for instance, accountants are all seen as unimaginative introverts or salesmen as hearty extroverts. The counsellor must be aware of these dangers if he is to have a genuine encounter with his client.

B. The concept of 'life-space' helps to ensure that the client is seen as a unique individual. The life-space is the psychological force-field which makes up the private and personal world of each of us. When two people meet in a counselling situation, it is the interaction between these forces which results in their actual behaviour. The concept of life-space can help to illuminate the counselling process.

1. Entering the life-space: The counsellor cannot force an entrance. He needs an invitation to be allowed in and it requires a climate of trust before the client will voluntarily lower his defences and allow the counsellor to enter his private world.
2. Behaviour within the life-space: Being allowed into another person's world is a privilege which should not be abused, and within the counselling process criticism is one such abuse. It is not only discourteous, but has the effect of stopping any effective counselling. The client feels threatened and starts to operate his defences.
3. Exploring the life-space: If the counsellor can help his client explore his own inner world, the client can more effectively examine and analyse what is worrying him. This may involve helping him to recall forgotten facts, look at his problem from a different angle or consider the implications of any intended action.

4. Dealing with emotions and feelings: A person's private world involves feelings and emotions as well as facts and events. Sensitive counselling helps people to get in touch with the feelings associated with their problem and this has a therapeutic effect.

5. Life-space, reality and fantasy: Fantasies are a normal part of everyone's life, helping, as they do, to minimise the harshness of the real world. But counselling can only be effective when the client is enabled to recognise and accept the facts that surround him and to discover realistic solutions.

6. Solutions that fit the life-space: Any new actions or changes which the client decides to make must be congruent with his basic personality and general outlook. Good counselling results in incremental change, rather than quantum jumps.

7. On leaving the life-space: In counselling, the way the meeting concludes is as important as the way in which it commenced. The client should feel that he has received real help and he should carry away with him a personal piece of work to do.

REFERENCES

Lewin, K., 'Need, Force and Valence in Psychological Fields,' in Hollander, E. P. and Hunt, R. G. (eds) *Classic Contributions to Social Psychology, OUP,* London, 1972

7

Developing the Organisation

As soon as people get together and form themselves into an organisation to do some work, a certain 'climate' is created between them. This climate, whilst hard to define precisely, can be felt by a visitor to the organisation and is of course experienced daily by those who work there. Go into any shop in the high street, and from the way you are served and treated, you will get a good idea of the shop's climate. The assistant may be warm and attentive, anxious to help without forcing goods on you. She may bring in one of her colleagues to help and you can judge from the way they work together, that they enjoy working there and that relationships are good. Enter another shop, and you may be met with indifference and a lack of courtesy, and there may be signs of tension among the staff. Clearly, the climate in these two shops is very different.

Every organisation, no matter what size it is, reveals its climate in many ways, some of which are obvious and others more subtle. For instance, the climate might be one in which authority and status are very important, and the ways in which things are organised continually underline this fact. There may be different dining rooms for different classes of people, different size cars symbolising rank, and even different lavatories. A climate in which these differences are continually emphasised must, in some way, affect the efficiency or profitability of the organisation.

Tradition plays a large part in characterising the climate of an organisation. The people who first worked there will have established ways of operating and behaving which suited them. These early methods and procedures become less and less appropriate over the years, but new employees are forced to accept these traditions as the price of membership, although they may be contrary to their own code of values or method of working. If they attempt to change them, they may be branded troublemakers and the organisation can exert a variety of pressures to make them conform.

This holds true for attitudes as well as methods, but attitudes are more difficult to analyse and define. If, for instance, an engineering company is losing orders and its share of the market, it may be relatively easy to recognise that the problem is one of poor product design and old machinery. It would be fairly simple to recommend that the company purchase modern equipment (given that the money was available) and to suggest improvements in the product design.

But the attitudes that exist in an organisation may be equally out-of-date and these have an even greater influence on overall performance. Attitudes of management to shopfloor workers, attitudes towards customers and the marketplace, and especially attitudes of employees to one another are all influenced by the organisation's climate and may reflect past economic or social situations that have long since changed. One important effect of an organisational climate which comprises inappropriate and outdated attitudes is that it fosters all the worst kinds of human feelings and emotions. This is due to the anxiety that is generated when people are forced to work in a climate that at best makes them feel uncomfortable or at worst, frightens and threatens them. Anxiety has a profound effect on behaviour at work, and the various psychological defences which anxious people operate can clearly be seen. In organisations the effects of these are hostility, suspicion, aggression, mistrust and bad relationships.

Successful organisations are those which can adapt to changing circumstances. It is a continuous and evolutionary process, and only those who change effectively survive. Those who fail to change become living fossils and die out. Here is the crux of the problem which faces every organisation in different degrees. On one hand, people in organisations establish patterns of work, attitudes and behaviour which harden into traditions and these are very difficult to change. On the other hand, the very existence of every organisation depends on its ability to develop and adapt itself to meet the constant changes in the environment.

The question that must be asked, therefore, by every manager is, how do you change organisations? There are a huge number of books on the subject and a new semi-science has developed called 'organisational development' which attempts to provide theories of change and to discover practical methods by which organisations can bring it about. Organisational development is still a very imprecise 'science' and perhaps, will necessarily always be so. It has had some success and has confirmed what many managers knew already from their own experience: namely, that attitudes and traditions are extremely difficult to change, especially at work.

An organisation should be able to produce its goods or services efficiently. If it encounters an obstacle, such as increased competition from a rival product or a cheaper service offered by a competitor, it should have the reserves and ability to respond quickly and effectively. A sudden or severe setback may result in a painful process of change involving drastic action, but a healthy organisation will fight back and achieve a full recovery.

To achieve this state of fitness, organisations require efficiency at all levels and a continual awareness of market changes. Few managers would disagree with this statement. The question is whether there is any particular part of an organisation which is vital to this state of health and which can contribute dramatically to the ability to respond quickly and appropriately to change. The answer surely is 'yes': the key area is located in the manager-subordinate relationship. Apart from marriage and the family, the manager-subordinate relationship is the most important relationship in the lives of people at work. Every manager has an effect on the performance of his subordinates and the way in which their work is carried out. Working with a 'good' manager can provide the subordinate with challenging and interesting work with all the range of feelings which result from stimulation and achievement. Such a manager gives appropriate feedback on performance and encouragement for promotion. The 'bad' manager is perceived as unhelpful and critical, perhaps behaving as an autocrat and creating fear and uncertainty.

The relationship a person has with his manager, whether good or bad, is bound to affect his performance and his feelings at work, and quite possibly, his behaviour outside work as well. A manager, similarly, worries about his subordinates and is affected by their behaviour. He may perceive them as good or bad, either eager to work and willing to take on responsibility or else lazy and uncooperative, avoiding work and careless of standards.

Perhaps the biggest effect of this relationship is in the growth and development of the subordinate. An effective manager is aware that the work a subordinate is given to do, together with the way he is treated, will either develop or constrict him. This is made more complex by the fact that the manager is in a position of authority and power over the subordinate. As Elliott Jaques says:

Here is an intensely human situation founded upon a

psychologically and emotionally subtle relationship. It is a social exchange relationship, the outcome of which affects the future success and progress of both the manager and the subordinate. It is not a simple economic exchange relationship. There is a complex underlay of hundreds of unspecified assumptions about appropriate modes of address and speech, giving of praise and criticism, special concessions, time off and special effort. *(A General Theory of Bureaucracy)*

Manager-subordinate relationships are at the heart of any organisation's effectiveness and the better these are, the healthier that organisation will be. After all, in every organisation, there are at least only one less manager-subordinate relationships than there are employees. That is to say, for every 1000 people employed in an organisation, at least 999 are involved in such a relationship. Clearly, the manager-subordinate relationship is very important to the subordinate, the manager and the organisation, and needs more exploration and explanation.

A useful way to proceed is through the idea of counselling: a good manager-subordinate relationship can be defined as a 'counselling relationship'. Counselling means helping, coaching and consulting, and although these activities may have to take place at times specified by the organisation, i.e. counselling at a formal appraisal interview, we are concerned here with an ongoing relationship in which these elements are continually present. There are of course problems in this approach. A good counsellor neither uses nor needs authority in his role, yet by definition a manager has authority over his subordinate. A counsellor helps the person being counselled to form his own solutions. However, a manager has targets, budgets and deadlines which have to be met, and these may have to override his subordinates' plans and his own.

These are real constraints and must be recognised as such, but they do not prevent a manager forming a counselling relationship with his subordinate to their mutual advantage. A clearer description of what this means in

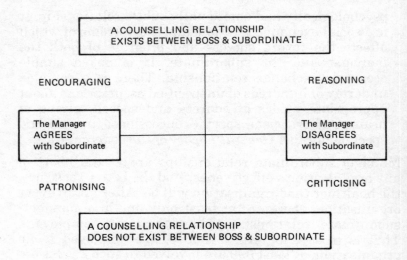

practice can be obtained by considering how a manager who has a counselling relationship with his subordinate behaves (a) when he agrees with his subordinate's action or plans and (b) when he disagrees. This can be compared with a manager in the same situations who does not have a counselling relationship.

The diagram illustrates the four basic behavioural styles a manager may use towards a subordinate, depending on whether a counselling relationship exists or not.

In a non-counselling relationship with his subordinates, the manager will *Patronise* when he agrees and will *Criticise* when he disagrees. But in a counselling relationship, the manager will *Encourage* when he agrees and *Reason* when he disagrees.

Patronising

The patronising manager is one who agrees with his subordinate's action, but does not have a counselling relationship with him. Consequently he is pleased, not so much with what the subordinate is doing, but with the fact that the subordinate is agreeing with him. It confirms his fantasy of god-like powers of creating someone in his own image, essentially a son or daughter whom he can be proud of. The patronising manager thinks in terms of rewards or punishments and when he is pleased, wishes to show this approval by giving some extra cash, or time off. Either way, the subordinate becomes conditioned to this kind of behaviour and tries increasingly to please the boss. And it becomes clear that what pleases the boss is acting more and more like him. The result is a subordinate who is not only a pale image of the manager, but is less and less himself and heavily dependent on his boss. His one aim is to please and, like a dog, he learns all the tricks that bring a reward. He learns not how to be an effective person but how to get the boss to open the biscuit tin.

Criticising

The criticising manager is one who disagrees with his subordinate's action and does not have a counselling relationship with him. He is essentially angry either openly or in a cold, controlled manner, because his own ideas of what is right or wrong have been challenged. Consequently the subordinate must be made to feel guilty and to experience his heavy displeasure in order to apologise and repent of his misdeeds. The critical manager will punish where he can, but where he has no open means of punishment, he will use his anger or else withdraw his friendship and affection. The re-establishment of relationships is a sign that the subordinate has been forgiven but also serves as a warning of what will happen if he errs again in the future. The result is a subordinate who spends a great deal of his time ensuring that his work and behaviour are in line with his boss's expectations and this can also involve his attitudes and opinions about the world in general. The dependence that this creates stifles initiative and encourages conformity and an over-regard for rules, regulations and procedures.

Reasoning

The reasoning manager is one who disagrees with his subordinate's plans or performance and has a counselling relationship with him. Instead of criticising, he explains the reasons for his disagreement and through direct questioning, helps the subordinate to face up to the facts of the situation and explore the likely consequences of his proposed action. The reasoning manager also has the humility to recognise that he is not the sole repository of truth and that a manager is not endowed with infallibility. Consequently, as he reasons with his subordinate he himself is open to the influence of fact and reason and may change his own mind, or modify his views. But if, at the end of it all, both remain unconvinced and the subordinate is still intent on a course of action with which the manager disagrees, the reasoning manager will take one of two courses of action. He may allow the subordinate to carry on, calculating that the risk involved is outweighed by the learning the subordinate may achieve by making a mistake. Or he may say 'no', repeat his reasons and exercise his legitimate authority. His right to do this stems from the fact that, in the last analysis, he is held accountable for his subordinate's performance. The outcome of this kind of behaviour is enormously valuable for the subordinate. He learns to evaluate his decisions and analyse the consequences of his actions. He learns how to use reason to state his case and argue his point. He learns to listen to another, and different, point of view and to modify and change his outlook without suffering a 'loss of face'. Most importantly, he learns from his manager how he might exercise his own authority in the future if he gets promotion. He is encouraged to be himself, to use to the full his own unique ideas and skills and at the same time, to recognise the genuine authority of his boss, without being frightened or unduly influenced by it. Finally, he also learns to recognise those issues which for him are vital, and where he must stand firm, even insisting on seeing a higher authority.

Encouraging

The encouraging manager is one who basically agrees with his subordinate's actions and who has a counselling relationship with him. He gives praise and congratulations and helps the subordinate to gain the maximum recognition for his successes. Although he ensures that there are the proper financial rewards for such efforts, he is equally concerned to see that his subordinate has further opportunities for future achievement. He tries to increase the subordinate's personal and professional development through increasingly challenging work, and balances new responsibilities with appropriate coaching and training. He shows his trust by delegating more of his own work to the subordinate and by involving him in increased consultation and decision-making. Finally, if he feels that the subordinate has outgrown his present job, he strongly recommends his promotion even though he will lose him. However, he believes that there are plenty of other good people around and he would like the chance to develop their potential. It is also likely that the encouraging manager will get promotion himself, because, of course, he now has a very suitable replacement.

CONCLUSION

Whilst formal counselling may take place at specified times during a year, its effectiveness depends on the quality of the relationship which exists the year round. The manager who is an effective counsellor has an attitude towards his subordinates which develops trust and openness between them at all times. The aim of the manager should be to build up a relationship which is not dominated by his greater authority, but is based on the essential characteristics of good human relationships. This is not to deny the real differences between a boss and his subordinate; it is to concentrate on the interdependence of the two roles and maximise co-operation and mutual assistance.

The strength of the boss-subordinate relationship is crucial to the effectiveness of the organisation, and directly affects its ability to change in response to new demands and situations.

SUMMARY

A. Every organisation develops a climate within it which consists of the unwritten rules which govern the ways in which people are expected to behave. This climate has a profound influence on everyone's behaviour and its acceptance is the price each person pays for his continuing membership.

B. An inappropriate climate, consisting of outmoded attitudes and traditions, can be as detrimental to an organisation's effectiveness as out-of-date plant and equipment. Every organisation must be able to adapt to meet changes in the environment if it is to be successful, but it is harder to change attitudes than machinery. The problem facing managers is how to maintain a stable organisation which at the same time has the flexibility to respond quickly to new circumstances.

C. The key to organisational flexibility lies in the manager-subordinate relationship. This relationship is at the heart of the organisation and has an effect on employees at every level, influencing not only their work performance but also their general morale.

D. An effective relationship between a boss and his subordinate can be characterised as a counselling relationship. This is demonstrated by the way they work together day by day, and it also enables the boss to counsel his subordinate when this is appropriate.

E. There are four basic behavioural styles which a manager may adopt towards his subordinate. These styles become apparent specifically when the manager agrees or disagrees with his subordinate. If there is not a counselling relationshp between them, the manager will Patronise when he agrees and Criticise when he disagrees. But in a counselling relationship he will Encourage when he agrees and Reason when he disagrees.

Patronising — The patronising manager behaves essentially as a father, proud that his child is following in his footsteps and agreeing with his own suggestions. As a result the subordinate tries more and more to please him and is in danger of becoming a 'yes-man'.

Criticising — The criticising manager becomes angry when he disagrees with his subordinate and will try to punish him. This creates fear and dependency in the subordinate who will then stick closely to rules and precedence in order to avoid any future penalties.

Reasoning — The reasoning manager explains why he disagrees but allows his subordinate to explain his point of view and argue his case. He is prepared to change his mind as a result of the discussion, but in the last analysis he is accountable for his subordinate's work and reserves the right to say 'no'.

Encouraging — The encouraging manager is pleased with his subordinate's performance and makes sure that he receives due recognition. Through delegation and appropriate training he encourages him to undertake greater responsibility and develop his own unique talents.

8

Anxiety And Stress At Work

Anybody who has ever tried to counsel, whether formally or informally, will have experienced anxiety – that sense of foreboding, the unpleasant feeling in the pit of the stomach, the fear that something unexpected will happen which will have an unpleasant effect.

In order to counsel effectively, it is essential for the counsellor to understand the nature of anxiety. Firstly, he must be able to recognise it in the person he is trying to help and this will enable him to understand that person's behaviour more clearly. Secondly, and perhaps more importantly, he must be able to recognise his own anxiety and the reasons for it, and be able to cope with it. Perhaps the most important characteristic of the effective counsellor is that he is able to contain his own anxiety. The most disastrous effect of anxiety on counselling is that it makes the counsellor want to do something, and takes him, from being client-centred, to being problem-centred. In these cases, the motive for his activity is not the well-being of the person being counselled, but the relief of his own anxiety. In many cases, simply to sit and listen without doing anything is extremely difficult and the more anxious one feels, the more difficult this becomes. But an understanding of the nature of anxiety and the ability to contain it are the hallmark of a mature counsellor and the prerequisite of helping.

THE NATURE OF ANXIETY

Anxiety is an intensely personal and subjective feeling. What is a challenge to one man may result in a nervous breakdown in another. Because anxiety is so basic and common, it can be too easily dismissed as merely part of the human condition. In fact, there are some managers who deliberately create anxiety in their departments. 'Keeps them on their toes. They never know where I'll hit them next.' This tendency can be seen especially in interviewing; some managers like to put interviewees under stress, to see how they cope. The results of such interviews are probably worthless.

But what causes this anxiety that is common to everybody and to all organisations? And what are its effects? And why should anxiety be singled out from the wide spectrum of human emotions as worthy of special consideration? One answer lies in the acute forms that anxiety can take. Most people will admit that some of their most unpleasant times have been when they have experienced acute anxiety. At a less intense level, a phone call from the boss's secretary saying that he wants to see you can create anxiety. The big conference where you have to make a speech can be terrifying; so, too, can the situation in which you have to tell some of your staff that they are redundant. These are specific experiences but you may also feel anxi-

ous for a whole variety of reasons that can be very difficult
to analyse, yet result in a general feeling of unease and
stress, which you carry around and which is extremely
hard to overcome and dissipate. Anxiety always creates
the same symptoms whether the cause is real or imaginery. The palms sweat, the heart pounds, blood pressure
increases and the bowels may be affected. If anxiety is
experienced as stress over a long period, then a whole
range of seemingly physical ills may result, ranging from
headaches and bad backs to high blood pressure, ulcers
and heart attacks. The explanation for these physical
responses to anxiety probably lies in the pre-history of
man. When primitive man was faced by a savage animal
or a hostile tribesman, he had only two courses of action
open to him for survival – fight or flight. To carry out
either of these strategies successfully required increased
strength and energy. The heart needed to beat faster to
carry oxygen to the muscles. Muscles were tensed, ready
for quick action. The bowels emptied to lose weight, and
adrenalin was pumped into the bloodstream ready to help
clotting if the person was wounded. The more this happened, the more likely our primitive ancestors were to
emerge successfully from fighting and overcoming the
enemy or running away from the threat. We respond to
danger in exactly the same way as our ancestors did half a
million years ago. Anxiety is man's response to danger.
This danger may be real or imaginery, but if he feels
threatened, for whatever reason, he will experience some
or all of the physical responses mentioned. If the danger is
obvious and immediate, he can still react in the old primitive way. For instance, if attacked by a young thug on the
way home, a man will automatically respond to this
danger by fighting to overcome the attacker, or by running away as fast as possible. People often describe how, in
these circumstances, they find a new strength and energy
which they didn't know they possessed. In fact, they used
the physical responses which anxiety automatically
brings out to overcome danger. But in modern society, and
especially in complex organisations, many anxieties are
caused by much more diffuse and imprecise dangers than

actual physical attacks, and the response of fight or flight
is impossible or inappropriate.

A manager in a large engineering group provides a good
illustration. A design engineer by training, he gradually
got promoted until he was made responsible for the new
computer systems department. But he knew little about
the use of computers and felt increasingly threatened by
the bright young graduates who were being recruited as
systems analysts. He couldn't express these fears either to
his colleagues, whom he imagined would accuse him of
incompetence, or to himself. Feeling threatened, he
became increasingly anxious and started to sleep badly
and have severe headaches. Eventually, he went to his
doctor, frightened that he had some dreaded disease, like
cancer or a brain tumour. Luckily he had a patient and
discerning GP, who helped the engineer to realise that the
origin of his illness was the anxiety he was experiencing
in his job. This example also helps to illustrate the nature
of acute stress. Acute stress is simply prolonged anxiety.
The bodily symptoms of anxiety originally evolved to
assist immediate survival action in a dangerous situation.
But if the dangerous situation continues over a long time
and cannot be resolved through fight or flight, the body
responds in the same way. Adrenalin will be continually
injected into the bloodstream, resulting in high pulse
rates and possible clotting and embolisms. Muscles continually tensed result in headaches and backaches. Blood
pressure may remain high, and all sorts of bowel and
stomach disorders may occur. Sexual potency may well be
affected, because a person feeling endangered is unlikely
to give much thought to sexual pleasure and procreation.

Problems which cause anxiety at work can be overcome
and mastered, provided they can be described and shared.
In other words, reality must be faced up to. Increasing
market share, developing new products, or improving a
company's cash flow position – problems of this sort are
part of the very nature of managing, and should not cause
acute anxiety.

But acute anxiety can arise from the areas of interpersonal relations and self-esteem, which are difficult to

describe and even more difficult to share. It can be very hard for a manager to face up to the reality that his job is too much for him; even harder, perhaps, to do something about it; harder, also, to resolve a situation where the boss appears autocratic and bullying. Even if the logical decision is flight – i.e. leave the organisation – economic and family pressures may make this impossible. Managers locked into large organisations are particularly vulnerable to feelings of anxiety, which, if unresolved, can develop into stress, with all its attendant ills and miseries.

So far, anxiety has been discussed in the context of some danger external to the individual, such as an attack by a thug, or working under an autocratic boss. In other words, situations in which there is real objective danger; the bad feeling which this causes is called 'objective anxiety'. But what about those occasions when people feel anxious for no obvious reason, that is when no objective fact seems to account for it? Everyone has memories and past experiences, fears and worries which are locked inside themselves and to which they do not wish to admit. These are all capable of creating anxiety, and if nothing is done about them, they can produce the unpleasant symptoms already described. Because these thoughts and fears arise from within, the feeling they produce is called 'neurotic anxiety'. So far as the individual is concerned, the anxieties are equally real. The most obvious defence against neurotic anxiety is called repression. Repression means burying the memory or fear as deeply as possible under the level of the conscious mind. There the anxious person hopes it will stay, out of sight and (apparently) out of mind. But, of course, it remains somewhere inside his head and will probably trouble him at some future date. Or it may sneak into his dreams.

Another personal defence mechanism is called projection. This is a subtle process. The mind tricks itself into believing that the cause of the anxiety is located in somebody else. For instance, a manager who has had a poor education may feel deeply envious and threatened by the young graduates entering the company whom he sees as cleverer and more able than himself. By using the process

of projection, the manager gets rid of his anxiety, changing 'I am envious of you' into 'You are envious of me'. He
can now begin to treat the graduates harshly, convinced
that these new boys want his job and are not prepared to do
a hard day's work.

'Forget all about that fancy college stuff. You won't
learn anything until you've got your hands dirty. I didn't
get where I am today by book-learning.' The source of his
anxiety is now (apparently) external and objective, and so
he can fight it. Small wonder if after 18 months the graduate leaves, fed up with boring jobs and being treated like
an idiot. This, of course, only confirms the manager in his
beliefs. 'There you are. They think the world owes them a
living. Not like it was in my day.' The real source of the
manager's anxiety, his feelings of being poorly educated,
remains with him, and unless it is dealt with, he is likely
to behave in exactly the same way to the next graduate.

Another example of projection is the person at work who
feels attracted to someone of his or her own sex. Such
feelings (perhaps more common than people care to admit)
may cause great anxiety. By using projection, the feeling
'I have homosexual feelings towards you' is transformed
into 'You have homosexual feelings towards me'. Again,
the source is now externalised, and so the person can
attack the other verbally or even physically, and show his
hatred of this disgusting behaviour. The real source of the
anxiety remains. It has been said that projection is the
basis for all moral indignation.

How does anxiety within people relate to that within
organisations? A whole range of outside factors can
threaten the organisation's survival, such as getting a
better market share, recruiting a good labour force,
increasing sales. All of these things can be tackled by
'fight or flight' behaviour. The sales director at the annual
conference says 'We're going to beat hell out of the opposition'. Competition in business can even be seen as stylised
warfare, played within certain rules, where there are
winners and losers.

But what of the feelings of anxiety which arise for
reasons within the organisation, like the neurotic anxiety

which arises from within the individual? An individual defends himself from these unpleasant feelings by such methods as repression and projection. What does an organisation do? There are three possible ways in which an organisation (or part of it, such as a department) can behave in an attempt to deal with internal problems which are causing intense anxiety and which it is unwilling or unable to face.

The first is *dependency:* people put their complete trust and hope in the leader. There is a general assumption that he, and he alone, will deliver the organisation out of all its problems without the need for any effort by others. Everyone else feels powerless and waits for the leader to achieve results as if by magic. Examples of the dependency mode of behaviour are legion, especially in politics. The members of a particular party place all their hopes in one person, believing against all experience and reason that this president or prime minister will usher in the golden age.

In industry and commerce, the same process occurs. The organisation faced with internal problems and difficulties appoints a new man and everyone waits to see what he will do. But what can the leader do? The internal problems can never be resolved simply by waiting for the leader to come up with the answer. In organisational terms, the problems which are causing the anxiety can only be resolved when they can be described and shared. This means hard work and analysis by everyone and involves the opposite of dependency – co-operation and mutual trust. If the leader can lead the organisation to work in this productive way, then the anxieties will diminish. But if the leader colludes in this fantasy that he alone can do it, then both he and the organisation are heading for trouble. Not only will he ignore the talents and abilities of his people, but he must inevitably fail in the role which he has accepted. The whole of history is littered with failed leaders who accepted this dependency role, and sooner or later failed to live up to the impossible expectations of their followers. Few dictators die peacefully; at a lower level, many whiz-kids brought in to save ailing companies last

only a very short time. The solution to internal problems
in organisations needs the application and co-operation of
all the members if the problems are to be confronted and
resolved. The 'dependency' leader may initially make
people feel all is well, but ultimately he will fail – and the
odium of failure will tarnish his reputation.

The second, related way in which an organisation may
behave to protect itself against internal anxiety is *messianic hope.'* A general assumption is made that soon
somebody or something will appear on the scene to deliver
everybody from all their troubles. 'Our economic problems
will be solved when North Sea oil comes on stream.' 'Once
we have the computer installed, we shall have no more
problems with invoicing customers.' Perhaps this particular defence against anxiety is seen best in the way some
firms use training departments or external consultants to
teach the 'latest thing'. Companies are full of the decaying
skeletons of management by objective schemes, which
were once believed to be the answer to low motivation and
achievement. T-groups, once thought to offer incomparable improvement in interpersonal relations, are now
viewed with the deepest suspicion. Blake and Moulton's
managerial grid with its scales leading up to maximum
concern for production on one axis and maximum concern
for people on the other is beginning to sound distinctly
old-fashioned.

This is not to be cynical about training. But managers
should distrust trainers and consultants who have the
answer at a price of £100 per head. Such false hopes will
always lead to cynicism and failure, because the anxieties
which arise from within the organisation are untouched
by these cosmetics. One very large company, which had
innumerable internal problems concerning both production and relationships, spent hundreds of hours and
thousands of pounds employing specialists to work on a
graduate recruitment scheme. The hope was that all problems would be solved by introducing bright young people
into every part of the company. It is doubtful if one per
cent have remained with that firm, which is now on the
verge of collapse. What was needed at that time was a

concentrated effort to straighten out production, regular-
ise supplies and improve the awful labour relations. The
company, which could not face up to these anxiety-
creating problems, misplaced its hopes on graduate
recruitment.

The third defence which an organisation may adopt
towards its internal anxiety is that of *'fight or flight'*
behaviour. Parts of the organisation fight against each
other, convinced that they are being 'got at' by head office
or that there must be a 'show-down' with the unions. This
fighting is essentially paranoic and inevitably results in a
depletion of energy.

Such behaviour throws up the worst sort of leader – one
who is convinced he is waging a holy war. Attacks are
entirely misdirected. Attacking head office through all
the manoeuvres known to management will not resolve
the root problems which are causing the anxieties. Again,
the only way forward is through the hard work and co-
operation of people in the organisation in an attempt to
face up to the real problems.

Anxiety is one of the main causes of inefficiency, both in
people and organisations. Because it is such an unpleasant feeling they are bound to develop ways of protecting
themselves from anxiety. In itself, protection can lead to
effective ways of behaviour: our ancestors survived the
various dangers they faced, through fight or flight
behaviour. But the causes of anxiety that come from
within the person or the organisation can lead to
behaviour that is both ineffective and wasteful of energy.
The more the individual resorts to repression and projection, the less energy he has with which to face reality and
live a normal and healthy life.

This is also true of organisations. The three modes of
behaviour described – dependency, 'messianic' hope and
fight/flight – all absorb energy. The more the organisation
behaves in these ways, the less energy there is available to
deal with the realities of cash flow, the changing market
and the proper aspirations of its employees. It will always
reveal hostility, rivalry and suspicion, and its social life,
as well as its business efficiency, will run down. On the

other hand, the more an organisation can minimise anxiety by helping its people to be in touch with what is really happening, both around them and within them, the more each individual is able to direct his mental energy towards his work and the aims of the company. Organisations which operate in this way are characterised by co-operation, and a climate which encourages the formation of relationships based on mutual trust and respect. Such a company, able to face up to the problems of its internal anxieties, will develop as an open system, able to regenerate itself and react appropriately to the constantly changing environment. Clearly, counselling can make a vital contribution to this process, enabling people to deal effectively with their problems and enabling the organisation to achieve its corporate goals.

SUMMARY

A. Anxiety is one of the most common unpleasant feelings which people experience. It is a reaction to a perceived threat and triggers off a number of physiological responses which enable a person to take effective action by overcoming or escaping from the danger. If anxiety is prolonged, it produces stress. When the automatic physiological responses cannot be channeled into effective fight or flight behaviour, they begin to damage the body, resulting in such symptoms as high blood pressure, headaches, backaches and stomach and bowel disorders.

B. Anxiety caused by a real threat, such as a physical attack, is called 'objective anxiety' and is reduced when the source of the threat is overcome or avoided. But what of the anxieties which arise from within the person himself, due possibly to past fears and memories? This is called 'neurotic anxiety' and is more difficult to deal with. People develop a number of psychological defences to cope with it, such as repression and projection, but neither deal effectively with the problem. Both objective and neurotic anxiety cause the same bodily reactions and in either case anxiety is reduced only when the root cause of the threat is faced and moved.

C. Anxiety affects organisations as well as individuals. The objective source of anxiety may come from increased competition or a reduction in sales and this causes the same fight/flight reactions. When this happens the organisation tries to overcome the opposition or take evasive action, through effective corporate strategies.

D. But what of the internal factors within the organisation which can give rise to anxiety, in the same way that an individual experiences neurotic anxiety? In this case, the interplay of the emotions and feelings of many people results in specific patterns of organisational behaviour which are essentially corporate defences against anxiety.

Three of these defences can be identified:

Dependency — In this mode of behaviour everyone puts
their trust in a leader and there is the general assumption that he, unaided, will deliver them from all their
troubles and problems. Everyone feels powerless and
there is a belief that the leader has limitless and almost
magical powers.

'Messianic' hope — In this instance, there is a general
assumption that some person or event will soon appear
on the scene which will solve all the organisation's
problems, such as North Sea oil, a new computer instal-
lation or the latest training package.

Fight or flight — This is not the legitimate fight against
competition but the fighting which occurs within the
organisation, such as fighting between the production
department and the sales office or between management and the unions.

E. These three modes of behaviour help people avoid coming to terms with the real issues within the organisation
which are making them anxious. They drain productive
energy away from the proper corporate objectives and
reduce efficiency. It is only when there is a climate of trust
and openness that everyone can communicate and share
their concerns and deal with the reality of organisational
life. Counselling, and the counselling relationship, can
make a significant contribution to this aim.

9

A Checklist For Counsellors

So far, this book has looked at different aspects of counselling in order to illustrate some of the processes which occur when counselling takes place. But counselling is essentially a practical piece of work where theories and ideas have to show themselves in effective performance. The following is a checklist which should help managers to carry out a good counselling interview.

1. What is the purpose of the interview?

Whenever possible, the manager should find time to consider the purpose of the interview. Of course this cannot happen when the meeting develops from some sort of crisis which finds a subordinate in distress. The reasons for the counselling interview may include all or some of the following:

(a) To help the interviewee let off steam;

(b) To help him to see himself or his problem more clearly;

(c) To support him while he finds his own solutions and makes his own decisions;

(d) To demonstrate interest and genuine concern.

It is a useful exercise to write down the following two statements: 'As a result of this interview, I hope that I will . . .' and 'As a result of this interview, I hope that he will . . .'.

2. What information do I need?

It has been known for a manager to commence his interview by saying 'Good morning Keith' only to hear the response 'Actually I'm Peter!' The manager must have as much information as possible concerning the person he is going to counsel. If it is an interview concerning performance appraisal, then he will want to know what happened at the previous interview and the significant achievements and failures of the subordinate's subsequent performance. The manager should take time to assimilate all the information and it is a good idea to make brief notes on a small piece of paper which can easily be referred to during the interview. It can be quite unnerving to the subordinate if the manager is continually burrowing into a file – the message comes over very clearly, 'I don't know much about you'.

3. Have I ensured privacy?

There are few things more counter-productive to a counselling interview than interruptions of any kind. The telephone must not be allowed to ring. If the manager is connected to his secretary's phone, then he can easily ask her not to put through any calls. Otherwise, the phone should be taken off the hook. People must be prevented from coming into the office by fixing a notice on the door saying 'meeting in progress'. Managers who do not have a room to themselves or else work in an office that is open-planned, must negotiate for a private room in which to hold the interview.

4. Where shall we sit?

There is no doubt that the physical arrangement of the room has a strong influence on the way in which a counselling interview proceeds. Most managers do their work sitting behind a desk and automatically take up that position when counselling a subordinate. But a desk may be much more than simply a useful piece of furniture for writing. It can also be a symbol of authority, which clearly indicates that he who sits behind it is more important than he who sits in front of it. It can also be a barrier, defining boundaries of privacy which must not be crossed. Counselling is likely to be more effective when both people sit facing each other on chairs of the same height without a desk between them, although a low coffee table may be useful for papers.

5. What time shall I need for the interview?

The first aspect of planning is time. When will you hold the interview? Have you allowed at least ten minutes before it so that you are relaxed and have time to refresh your memory of the facts? And, perhaps more importantly, how long have you allowed for the interview itself? This will of course depend on how busy you are and the importance you give to the subject under discussion. But it is unlikely that less than half an hour will be sufficient and probably not more than an hour will be needed. Having decided on the length of the interview, it is important that the manager informs the subordinate of this at the outset. Finally, have you allowed at least quarter of an hour between the end of the interview and your next engagement? This time is needed to reflect on what has happened and to make any notes. It also ensures that the manager does not spend the last ten minutes of the interview looking at his watch and mentally preparing for the next appointment.

6. What is the best plan for the interview?

A counselling interview needs to be properly managed if it is going to be useful, and it requires appropriate direction by the manager. This can only happen if the counsellor prepares an outline plan which makes full use of the time available. One basic approach is 'WASP' where W=welcome, A = acquiring information, S = supplying information, P = parting. Skilful planning of the interview ensures that the counselling process is completed within the allotted time.

7. How shall I start the interview?

Interviews have been described as 'a conversation with a purpose'. When a conversation begins, it is usual for the people involved to talk about such seemingly irrelevant matters as the weather, sport or the state of each other's health. But these opening gambits have a real purpose – they set the scene and establish an initial rapport which facilitates the discussion of more important matters to follow. The same is true in commencing an interview. The manager must welcome his subordinate and set the scene in which an appropriate counselling interview can ensue. The more the subordinate can feel relaxed and at ease, the more he will speak openly and frankly about his attitudes and feelings. Getting down to business too soon can result in the subordinate feeling tense and apprehensive.

8. What kind of relationship do I want to establish?

The relationship established in a counselling interview is bound to reflect the day-to-day relationship which already exists between the manager and his subordinate. If the normal relationship is slightly cold and remote, then the manager will have to work very hard to establish a warmer and more friendly atmosphere. On the other hand, too much *bonhomie* from the manager, especially if this is unusual, may worry the subordinate and make him wonder if he is being softened up before hearing the bad news. The best relationship is one in which both parties feel at ease and can behave naturally and feel able to speak openly and honestly. It should also be such that it contributes to the future working relationship.

9. What information needs to be exchanged?

Counselling depends on getting down to the facts, although initially what may be fact to one may not seem true to the other. If you are counselling on performance, then you must have as much fact as possible about what your subordinate has achieved and the way he has gone about his work. If there are failures you should be especially sure of your facts and be able to present these to the subordinate in a non-threatening way. After all, the aim of counselling is to find ways of overcoming problems such as poor performance, and not to play the role of sentencing judge. Part of the information you may have to convey may be bad news, such as failure to achieve a pay rise or a promotion. The important thing here is to give the reasons and also to take responsibility for your decision. A subordinate can feel very nonplussed if he is told that 'they' have refused an application for promotion. But if he is told that you have made this decision and for the following reasons, then he can discuss it with you (he may even get angry) and discover what he should do to improve his chances in the future. Or, and this may be the most difficult, he may realise that he has no future chances for

promotion, and counselling can help him to come to grips
with this reality.

10. What kind of questions should I ask?

Invariably in counselling, the open-ended question is the
best kind to ask. An open-ended question is one which
allows the client the maximum choice in his reply and
enables him to explore his own reactions to the full. Such
questions could be:

> 'Would you like to tell me more about that?'
> 'Why do you say that?'
> 'What did you do then?'
> 'What are you going to do now?'
> 'If you go ahead and do that, what do you think will be
> the consequence?'

The opposite type of questioning produces from the subordinate 'yes' or 'no' answers.

11. How can I help him explore his feelings?

In any counselling interview the manager must encourage his subordinate to express his feelings. By his
behaviour and the nature of their relationship, he must
indicate that this is perfectly legitimate and acceptable.
The manager must be prepared to experience his subordinate's emotions, such as sadness or anger, and his own
emotions. A counselling interview without the expression
and experience of feelings can never be fully effective. The
classic question to ask is simply 'How did that make you
feel?' or to deal with the immediate situation, 'How are
you feeling now?'. Dealing with feelings is especially
important when people come to you with a personal problem and request an interview; the effective counsellor
knows that on these occasions, emotions and feelings are
always part of the problem. Their expression is frequently
therapeutic and contributes directly to resolving the particular problem.

12. How can I ensure that appropriate action will be taken?

An effective counselling interview will frequently end with one or both parties agreeing to take some particular action. For the subordinate, this may be something very practical, and the manager should make certain that they both agree on this and understand how it will be achieved. The subordinate may agree to do something less tangible, involving changes in attitude or personal behaviour. The manager also frequently agrees to take some action. But he must be careful. Good counselling can often be exhilarating for both people concerned, with a real sense of achievement and the pleasure of human relationship. The manager must be careful not to promise what he cannot fulfil or what is outside of his authority or company policy. In the 'supplying information' stage, he may need to state clearly company policy so that any action which is taken is within the boundaries of his authority and overall company policy.

13. How shall I conclude the interview?

The way in which an interview is concluded is as important as the way it commences. Those last words spoken, the warmth of the final handshake, all leave a flavour which will remain as significant memories in the subordinate's mind. Careful management of time is important so that completion of counselling work coincides with the end of the allocated time period. The last five minutes are best used for a recapitulation of what has been agreed and especially what action both parties have agreed to take. It also provides an opportunity to ensure that the relationship is sound, especially if strong words have been exchanged during the interview. The aim is for both parties to come from the interview feeling that problems have been resolved and that mutual understanding has been increased.

SUMMARY

1   Determining the purpose of the interview:
    What do you want to achieve?
2   Preparation for the interview:
    Have you got all the information you need concerning
    your subordinate?
3   Ensuring privacy:
    Have you made certain that you will not be inter-
    rupted?
4   Seating arrangements:
    Are the chairs in the best position?
5   Planning the time:
    Have you allowed enough time before your next
    appointment?
6   Planning the structure of the interview:
    Have you made an outline plan for the interview?
7   Starting the interview:
    How will you begin so that you will set the client at
    ease?
8   Establishing a counselling relationship:
    How friendly do you want to be?
9   Exchanging information:
    Have you got all the facts and information you may
    need to give?
10 Asking the appropriate questions:
    Have you considered some open-ended questions you
    might ask?
11 Exploration of feelings:
    Are you prepared to allow him to express his feelings?
12 Concluding the interview:
    Have you thought about how you will finish the
    interview?
13 Taking appropriate action:
    Are you prepared to follow up the interview with
    appropriate action?

Appendix I: Training For Counselling

For many people, counselling can be a frightening thing to contemplate doing, simply because they have never received any training for it. At work, counselling skills are one of a number which managers are supposed to 'pick up' as they climb the ladder of promotion. Fortunately, many people are realising that management is a collection of knowledge and skills which can be studied and learnt but there are still too many organisations where technical skills are taken as signs of management potential and that it is the best technicians who are promoted. Of course, common sense, intelligence and the ability to learn from experience can help people to become good managers. But the ability to counsel effectively is unlikely to be acquired in this way. Since counselling can make a powerful contribution to developing both personal

and organisational effectiveness, then training in counselling skills is vital to anyone who is responsible for the
work of others.

For the past ten years I have been involved in helping
managers develop their counselling skills and I have
developed a training method which is effective. It is certainly not original, but it is simple and I pass it on in the
hope that others may benefit from it.

GENERAL SITUATION

The ideal method requires one tutor to each group of three
trainee counsellors. The tutors should be people who have
a good understanding of counselling from both a practical
and a theoretical standpoint and who are also good
teachers – a combination not always easy to find! The total
number of people who could attend such a programme
clearly depends on the number of competent tutors
available, but where possible, I like to work with a group
of 12 trainees – and we therefore require a total of four
tutors.

A room is needed big enough to allow all the tutors and
trainees to sit down comfortably together and where there
is a flipboard or blackboard. There also needs to be room
for each group to work separately in total privacy. On
residential courses, bedrooms are often used for this purpose.

STARTING THE PROGRAMME

The purpose of the day

The tutor who is directing the training should welcome
the trainees and, after making any necessary administra-

tive points, state very clearly the purpose of the day. I find it remarkable that people can organise training courses without being certain what their teaching objectives are. I find it even more remarkable that people attend courses equally uncertain why they are there or what their own learning objectives are. Anyone organising counselling training must make sure that in any written material sent out before the course the purpose of that course is stated clearly and unambiguously. This must also be spelt out at the start of the day and written up so that it is clearly seen by everyone.

I use the term 'primary task' and the following form of words: 'The primary task of this training day is to provide members with the opportunity to understand, learn and practise the skills which are necessary for effective counselling.' I then say, half-jokingly, that if anyone does not want to do this, then now is the time to leave. So far, no one has walked out, but it does make the point that we now have a contract between us, and as we shall see later, this enables tutors and trainees to play their proper roles.

The tutor's role

The directing tutor will then outline the programme, pointing out that later on the trainees will be working in trios, each trio having its own tutor. At this stage he will introduce the tutors and briefly describe their role. Their role, when working with the trios is that of consultant, which is a variant of counsellor. They are there, not to teach or instruct, but to act as catalysts in the learning situation. In essence, their role is to maximise the learning for each individual. (It goes without saying that all the tutors will have met beforehand and discussed and agreed their role.)

The 'ice-breaker' exercise

Counselling training requires a climate of trust and openness if it is to be effective. Anyone coming on a training day – especially one dealing with interpersonal skills – is likely to feel anxious and apprehensive at the start. What are the other people like? Are they friendly? Will I make a fool of myself? Will it be worth the time involved? If I was sent on this course, does it mean I have poor social skills? All these questions are likely to be in the minds of the trainees and it is essential that these fears and worries are reduced before any proper training begins. For this reason, I start with an 'ice-breaking' exercise, which is commonly used on a variety of training courses.

The trainees are invited to pair up with someone they don't know (or with the person they know least well), find a quiet corner somewhere and then interview each other with the purpose of finding out as much as they can about one another. I always invite them to try to discover information not only about each other's job and interests, but also why they have come on this training day and what they hope to get out of it. The interviews last a quarter of an hour each, so that this exercise lasts for half an hour. It is usually very effective. The trainees becomes transformed from a quiet and apprehensive group of strangers into a number of pairs who are talking animatedly to each other.

After this half hour, the trainees resume their original seats and then each is given two minutes to introduce the person they have been interviewing to the rest of the group. Of course, people start to ask questions and slowly the anxiety begins to disappear as they realise that the others are not so different from themselves and that they share many common problems and interests.

THE LECTURE

Following the 'ice-breaker' exercise, a tutor gives a lecture of about 30 minutes, in which he outlines the purpose and method of counselling. It is essential that the trainees understand the theory of counselling: I am a great believer in the dictum of Kurt Lewin 'There's nothing so practical as a good theory!' Every tutor will have his own approach and will want to emphasise those points which he thinks are particularly important. If the tutor can make four strong points in his 30-minute lecture, he will be doing well. As an example, here are the headings from the lecture I give; in practice, of course, I vary this a great deal, depending on my audience and how I am feeling at the time.

Outline Lecture Notes

1. *The purpose of counselling —*
   to help a person examine and solve his own problems
2. *What hinders counselling? —*
   closed questions
   too much talking by the counsellor
   giving advice
   criticism.
3. *What helps counselling? —*
   active listening
   open and reflective questions
   a relationship of trust and openness
   the recognition of the person as being important.
4. *The value of counselling —*
   it reduces anxiety and worry
   it increases personal growth and development
   it increases the effectiveness of the subordinate
   it increases the effectiveness of the department and
   the organisation.

I then allow half an hour for questions and discussion, in which all of the tutors take part.

THE COUNSELLING EXERCISE IN TRIOS

Selecting a real problem

There can be little doubt that the more realistic the training situation can be made, the more learning will be acquired. It is for this reason that I invite trainees in counselling to bring with them a real problem that is currently concerning and worrying them and about which they would like some help. There is of course no way in which anyone can be forced to reveal a problem which they would otherwise have kept hidden, but one can certainly encourage people to be brave and bold. I also say that, as far as possible, the problem should be work related. Initially some people are taken aback and are clearly concerned by this request. Those who find this idea too threatening are told that they can make up a problem or bring one that they used to have. But I also point out that past or imaginery problems can never have the emotional content which a real, current problem generates, and, to that extent, it will not be a good training vehicle. I add that whilst the aim of the exercise is to give people an opportunity to practise their counselling skills, there is a bonus in that the person presenting the problem is very likely to receive real help.

Briefing for the counselling exercise

The directing tutor now describes the procedure for carrying out the counselling exercise in the trios:

Each exercise commences with a counselling interview in which Mr A is the counsellor, Mr B is the client and Mr C is the observer. The tutor plays the role of consultant. This interview should last for approximately 15 minutes, during which time the observer remains perfectly quiet and unobtrusive. The next stage is for the observer to recount what he has seen and to evaluate the performance of the counsellor. The counsellor and client may well wish to join in the debate and the aim should be for Mr A to learn as much as he can about how well he performed and to see where and how he might make improvements. At the same time, the other two will also be learning and considering what this means for them. The evaluation and learning stage is crucial, and could last up to half an hour. The process of interview and evaluation is then repeated twice so that each member of the group has played each of the three roles.

The tutor will conclude his briefing by saying that he realises that the person in the counselling role is unlikely to complete the counselling in 15 minutes, but that this is long enough for the purposes of training and will provide plenty of information for discussion and learning. He may add that if the interview overruns its time, the observer could give a pre-arranged signal, such as a tap on the chair, so that things can be brought to a conclusion.

Carrying out the counselling exercise

When the three people have assembled in their room, the tutor will briefly check with them to see if they have understood their instructions. He may help them to agree on the batting order and the placing of chairs.

The tutor will usually keep silent, like the observer, during each of the interviews, and make his comments during the evaluation periods. However, he may occasionally have to intervene with a comment during an interview if people are getting out of role or in the unlikely instance that things are going wildly wrong.

During the evaluation period which follows each interview, the tutor has a vital role to play and he must remember his objective, which is to maximise the learning for each member of the trio. One of his main tasks will be to help the observer keep to his proper role of analysing and evaluating the performance of the interviewer. The problems presented are frequently so fascinating and absorbing that the observer is caught up in them and wants to give his own solutions or criticise those that have been discussed. This can result in a very likely discussion, but it is at the expense of the learning. The tutor must gently but firmly point out what is happening and help the observer return to his proper job.

The other task the tutor will have, especially in the first evaluation period, is to raise important points which the observer may have missed. Each evaluation period should include at least the following points:

(a) How did the interview commence?
(b) What kind of relationship was established?
(c) How well were questions used?
(d) Who did most of the talking?
(e) Was the core of the problem revealed?
(f) Were feelings expressed?
(g) Was any advice given?
(h) Did the client feel criticised?
(i) Did the client receive real help?

The effective tutor enhances the exercise not only by contributing to the interview evaluation, but by his own behaviour, because he is in fact acting as counsellor to the group. The performance of each subsequent interview thus clearly improves and the final one is substantially better than the first.

THE FINAL PLENARY DISCUSSION

Following the trios, all the trainees and tutors meet together to discuss their experiences. The tutor should at the start make it clear that this is not the place to discuss the actual problems which were presented in the trios, but rather how they found the actual process of counselling. This again can be a vital stage in the learning process as people try to come to grips with their recent experiences and discover what they must do to improve their own skills.

That each person learns something different is evident from the variety of points that arise at this final session. The hearty, talkative type will learn that it may be better if he can listen rather than speak all the time. The tentative, shy person may grow to realise that with a little more confidence, he can ask direct, pertinent questions that will make him more effective. Others may realise that their manner does not invite confidences and wonder what they can do about it. Yet others may have learnt that they criticise too much and that this antagonises people.

If the day has gone well, all the people attending will have learnt something about themselves and more importantly, about the most valuable skill of helping and counselling a fellow human being.

Appendix II: Further Reading

A. Counselling, consulting and the therapeutic process: some theories, explanations and practical guides.

Axline, V., *Dibs — In Search of Self,* Pelican Books, Harmondsworth, 1973. (A beautifully written true account of the therapy which enabled a boy to find himself)

Clare, A.W. and Thompson, S., *Let's Talk About Me. A Critical Examination of the New Psychotherapies,* BBC, London, 1981.

Dean, H and Dean, M., *Counselling in a Troubled Society,* Quartermaine House, 1981.

Dickson, J.D. and Roethlisberger, F.J., *Counselling in an Organisation,* Harvard University, 1966. (An account of the Hawthorne counselling programme)

Kennedy, E., *On Becoming a Counsellor — A Basic Guide for Non-professional Counsellors,* Gill and Macmillan, 1977.

Kovel, J., *A Complete Guide to Therapy,* Penguin Books, Harmondsworth, 1978.

Lippet G. and Lippet, R., *The Consulting Process in Action,* University Associates, California, La Jolla, 1978.

Patterson, C.H. *Theories of Counselling and Psychotherapy,* Harper & Row (3rd edn.), London 1980.

Rogers, C.R., *Client Centred Therapy,* Constable, 1965.

Schein, E., *Process Consultation,* Addison-Wesley, Reading, Mass., 1969.

Venables, E., *Counselling,* National Marriage Guidance Council 1971, reprinted 1975.

Principles of Counselling, BBC Further Education, London, 1978.

B. Theories and explanations of individual and interpersonal behaviour and development.

Argyle, M., *The Psychology of Interpersonal Behaviour,* Penguin Books, Harmondsworth, 1970.

Bion, W.R., *Experiences in Groups,* Tavistock Publications, London, 1968.

Jung, C.G., *The Undiscovered Self* (trans. by R.F. Hull), Routledge & Kegan Paul, London, 1974.

Rogers, C.R., *On Becoming a Person,* Constable, London, 1961.

Salzberger-Wittenberg, I., *Psycho-Analytic Insight and Relationships — A Kleinian Approach,* Routledge & Kegan Paul, London, 1970.

Storr, A., *The Integrity of the Person,* Pelican Books, Harmondsworth, 1960.

The Seven Ages of Man, New Society Reprint, first published as a series of articles in 1964.

C. Organisational behaviour – Ways in which people behave at work.

Clifton Williams, C., *Human Behaviour in Organisations,* South-Western Publishing Co., 1978.

de Board, R., *The Psychoanalysis of Organisations,* Tavistock Publications, London, 1978.

Handy, C.B., *Understanding Organisations,* Penguin Books, Harmondsworth, 1976.

McGregor, D., *The Human Side of Enterprise,* McGraw-Hill, New York, 1960. (A classic, explaining the famous Theory X and Theory Y)

Schein, E., *Organisational Psychology,* Prentice-Hall, Englewood Cliffs, NJ, 1965.

D. Transactional analysis.

Berne, E., *Games People Play,* Grove Press Inc., 1964; Penguin Books, Harmondsworth. 1968.

Berne, E., *What Do You Say After You Say Hello?,* Bantam Books, 1973.

James, M. and Jongeward, D. *Born to Win,* Addison-Wesley, Reading, Mass., 1971.

Jongeward D. *Everybody Wins: Transactional Analysis Applied to Organisations,* Addison-Wesley, Reading, Mass., 1973.

Klein, M., *Lives People Live,* John Wiley & Sons, New York, 1980.

Wagner, A. *The Transactional Manager,* Prentice-Hall, Englewood Cliffs, NJ, 1981.

E. Understanding health and stress.

Gillie, O. and Mercer, D., *The Sunday Times Book of Body Maintenance,* Michael Joseph, London, 1978.

Melhuish, A., *Executive Health,* Business Books, London, 1978.

Open University, *The Good Health Guide,* Harper & Row, London, 1980.

The BMA Book of Executive Health, Times Books, London, 1979.

Index